# journey
## of a
# red soul

by Marie Dion

BALBOA
PRESS
A DIVISION OF HAY HOUSE

Balboa Press books may be ordered through booksellers or by contacting:

Balboa Press
A Division of Hay House
1663 Liberty Drive
Bloomington, IN 47403
www.balboapress.com
1 (877) 407-4847

Because of the dynamic nature of the Internet, any web addresses or links contained in
this book may have changed since publication and may no longer be valid. The views
expressed in this work are solely those of the author and do not necessarily reflect the views
of the publisher, and the publisher hereby disclaims any responsibility for them.

The author of this book does not dispense medical advice or prescribe the use of any
technique as a form of treatment for physical, emotional, or medical problems without the
advice of a physician, either directly or indirectly. The intent of the author is only to offer
information of a general nature to help you in your quest for emotional and spiritual well-
being. In the event you use any of the information in this book for yourself, which is your
constitutional right, the author and the publisher assume no responsibility for your actions.

Print information available on the last page.

ISBN: 978-1-5043-9253-2 (sc)
ISBN: 978-1-5043-9255-6 (hc)

Library of Congress Control Number: 2018911294

Balboa Press rev. date: 10/25/2018

It was 2003 when an intense, charming, and lively Marie Dion came to my office with a request to help her family clear some negative energy from their home. It turned out to be one of the more challenging and interesting "cases" that I have ever done, showing me how layers of family history and our past life history can be intertwined and effect us powerfully for generations.

We got to the bottom of it eventually, which you will read all about in this book! Once the issues were resolved, I remember standing in the parking lot of my office with Marie when she said, "We are going to be friends for a long time and help each other." It was a prophetic statement for sure, and I felt my heart ring like a bell when she said it, as I do when someone speaks a deep truth.

And it has been true. It's been my pleasure to witness Marie open to her psychic ability and her spiritual nature, learning how to connect with and trust her guides so that she now lives seamlessly with one foot in the world of Spirit and the other very practically in the sacred ground of her farm.

My work has always been to train psychics, healers, and sensitives to fully master their gifts so that they can step into their life purpose, since I believe more than anything that the world needs all the healers that it can get! I am a long time teacher of Reiki and psychic development classes as well as the Dean of Students at an Energy Healing Institute in the Boston area. I also have a busy private practice doing psychic readings, energy healing sessions, and spiritual counseling and am now the author of the book about Psychic Reiki whose beautiful illustrations are all Marie's work!

Marie and I have supported each other personally and professionally for over 15 years. Her artwork hangs in my house, and I would let no other designer work with my business. It has been my honor to be a part of Marie's spiritual development, and a pleasure to show up as a character in this book!

*Journey of A Red Soul* emerges from the heart of a storyteller, and I know for a fact that Marie's primary guide, whom she calls "Grandfather," woke her in the early hours of the morning and told her to start writing the story of her journey. It's a powerful, moving, and entertaining story of discovery and healing. It is her journey of learning to trust her guidance and to heal the past wounds of her biological family, her own past-life history, and also the wounds of an entire race of people: the Native Americans.

Since I have known her, she has always claimed her Native heritage with pride and love — living, as she says, with a red soul. *Journey of A Red Soul* is about healing the pain and fragmentation of her personal past, genetically and karmically. It is now being shared with you and the world in the hopes of bringing healing to the wounds of the Native people and to the white folks who have adopted this country, with great and horrible consequence to the people that were already here. It is not an accident that much of this work was written during the stormy time of the Standing Rock protest. Our country needs to heal its past with the First People for us all to prosper, and much work needs to be done here.

Let us hope that hearing each other's stories might be the first step to forgiveness, understanding, and healing. *This book is a courageous step in that process.*

*Journey of A Red Soul* is also a personal healing story for Marie, as she shares with courage, vulnerability, and honesty the lessons she has learned through her family and personal relationships and the evolution of her spiritual and artistic gifts. Woven through this narrative are her past life memories and the healing that takes place as she works through painful karmic wounds, bringing them into the light.

Most of all, *Journey of A Red Soul* is a book about hope and healing, and you are in for a treat as you begin your journey with this book.

Jayne Gabrielle
*Psychic Counselor and Reiki Master Healer*

soft light in four directions                                        2005

# a red soul  poem by Marie Dion

I have a story to tell...
    a red soul will understand
    a red soul remembers all
    a red soul has returned

I have a story to tell...
    do I look white to you?
    have I blended in well?
    have I been controlled, conquered, eradicated?
    no. I am still here, it is still me.

I have a story to tell...
    my children who were murdered in my arms
    now surround me in "this" life
    my tribe scattered, have now gathered once again
    we are here together
    for our mother, the earth, for ourselves,
    to heal what's been done

I have a story to tell...
    can you hear, can you see?
    many years we were not heard, we were not seen...
    can you hear us now? can you see us now?
    we are still here

*I have a story to tell…*
 *are we still in your way? as you take "all" that we have*
 *what of the treaties you so desperately wanted us to sign?*
 *you do not honor any of them, you have no honor.*
 *it made no sense to us then it makes no sense to us now,*
 *as you destroy our mother earth, you destroy yourselves*

*I have a story to tell…*
 *our ties to our ancestors are strong,*
 *their wisdom flows through us,*
 *we listen*
 *we are still here*
 *a healing from what's been done needs to occur.*
 *as we heal, as we forgive, those who came before or*
 *those yet to come…*
 *will heal… seven generations*

*I have a story to tell…*
 *of a red soul's journey to heal what was done,*
 *what has happened, forgive?*
 *we must, we are here to do so,*
 *we have returned for our mother, we are here among you*
 *those of us with red souls*

*We have a story to tell…*
 *do you have ears to hear, eyes to see?*
 *or are you as blind and deaf as your ancestors were?*
 *taking what was not theirs to take.*
 *there is still a story that must be told for all of us to heal*
 *red, white, yellow, and black*

*May healing happen for all…*
 *may all your stories be told and acknowledged,*
 *may forgiveness and healing surround you and those you love*
 *for the good of all and harm to none, aho!*

One afternoon last winter I had a Native friend stop by for a visit. She shared a poem with me that she had written, and as she read her words, I could feel her ancestors speak through her. An unmistakable chill ran through me as a sign of confirmation, and I heard from Spirit, "The time has come!" I had no idea what the significance of this acknowledgment was but it was a powerful moment for both her and I. When I awoke the next morning, the poem featured in the introduction of this book came to me from Spirit, word for word.

Why was I chosen to bring the message of the poem and this book? I don't know. I'm only the vessel through which it came. This information flows through me but I do not own it. What this means, I do not fully understand just yet. Every day more is revealed as I listen and am instructed by those I call my ancestors. This instruction has taken place throughout my life, before culminating in the channeling of this poem and the decision to write this book. What Spirit has revealed to me, through personal past-life experiences and shared stories, creates a broad picture of how we return to life again and again to experience the world from different perspectives. We have the chance to either heal and grow, or fail to learn and inflict harm on others. Which of these scenarios occurs depends on the choices we make, and the consequences manifest in this life and our lives to come.

Let me tell you a story from long ago that my ancestors shared with me — one of many that happened during the initial occupation of the Americas.

There was a settler, a white man who hated the Natives. He did not listen when he was told by the U.S. government what land belonged to the Native people through treaty agreements. He initially obliged, but after weeks and months of staring, frustrated, at the rich ground lying fallow across the river, he eventually decided for himself that they weren't even using the land and it was being wasted. He did not understand that the Native way of 'using' land is being in a relationship with the land and having a deep spiritual connection to it and our Mother Earth. In his arrogance, the settler decided that he would claim the land on the other side of the river for his ranch, even if doing so was in direct contradiction to the U.S. government's treaty. He settled himself on the wrong side of the river, establishing his ranch on Native land. From that moment on, he proceeded to murder any Native he saw traveling through on horseback and crossing land he now claimed as his. He hid and shot unsuspecting Native men, women, and children with his shotgun, killing them off their horses without warning and without remorse. He took what was not his and treated other human beings without respect or compassion. He treated everyone besides himself as if they were animals. With no regard for women of any race, he raped, abused and murdered them at every opportunity.

So, in his next life, he was reborn on a reserve as a Native woman who was abused similarly to how he had abused others. He was not allowed to come back into his position of power as a white male, and had to experience a life subject to the abuse he had perpetrated on others. He had never lived a lifetime as a Native person and now his soul came back with the intention to heal his arrogance and prejudice by experiencing the opposite perspective. The beliefs of his prior life needed to be healed in this new lifetime so that compassion could settle in his heart and he could become a better human being. This lifetime's experience as a Native woman offered him true understanding of the Native way. His heart shed its prejudice and reached a place of soul healing.

And what of those who were hurt or killed by this white man in his first life? Who do you think they came back as? Many, myself included, came back to experience a "white" lifetime so they could also heal the hate, pain, anger, and prejudice that had become a part of them because of the white man's actions. In experiencing "the other" in this deep way, true and transformative forgiveness is possible.

This is why judgment of another serves no purpose. We can never know another's journey, or see the entire complexity of the person standing before us. What any one individual can overcome in a single lifetime is miraculous. They have the potential to become whole, loving, and peaceful, no matter who they were in times before. Creator has given us everything we need to accomplish this within ourselves. Our own journey is not like the journey of any other person that stands next to us, no matter how similar they seem to be. We are each unique in the combinations of lifetimes we have experienced. Whether we are a new, young soul or an old soul that has been here tens of thousands of times, we each eventually experience our own version of the same lessons, in the same way we share common experiences as children who grow and learn together in a classroom or community. We do not judge a three-year-old because she cannot accomplish the same things as a twenty-year-old. We know that in time that child will learn. Are you the same as you were five years ago? Ten years ago? Thirty years ago? When you look at other people, know that they are changing just as much as you are.

There is a universal law of cause-and-effect in each of our lives that we are not able to escape. Just as boundaries need to be set for children at each stage of their lives so they can grow in safety, self-worth and good self-esteem, souls' journeys are governed by this cause-and-effect principle. When the boundaries for growing children are not set, the child suffers and has to recover and heal from the pain. Likewise, when the lessons are not learned on the soul's journey, it suffers and has to recover and heal by experiencing the opposite perspective.

When we cross over from one life to the next, we experience a life review. Since we are all so used to watching TV, many people envision the experience to be something like that, but this is not so. Your life review, from what I understand from the spirits, is you standing in the place of the other, experiencing all that you have done to them and the emotions of pain or joy that they experienced from your actions. If you were loving or abusive, you will experience the consequences of either in the same way those you affected in life felt them. This is what is meant when the elders say to try to imagine life as if standing in another's shoes, because when your life review happens, you are responsible for the experience you have to endure. Will it be a joyful or painful experience for you? Jesus' teaching of "do unto others as you would have them do unto you" is the same teaching, just as in the Christian tradition. The clarity of this when you finally experience and understand it is immense, especially because none of us are perfect.

As much as we try to teach our children not to make the same mistakes we did, they will inevitably continue to do so, because they have to experience the mistake in order to learn the lesson that comes from it. It is the same for all of us spiritually, and our experience in this lifetime on earth is a gift to help us accomplish this. Each lifetime is full of potential to fulfill our souls' deepest yearnings. To conquer our fear and experience a life that fulfills our soul's objective is what will bring us the most joy and fulfillment. To heal from all the mistakes we have made and move forward without looking back is what allows us to become better human beings. This way, when it comes time for our life review, we don't have to feel the suffering and pain that we have inflicted on others. Instead, we get to feel love and joy, and witness all of our life's successes and our own growth. Can you imagine how happy your soul will feel having done this? It is the same as the fulfillment you experience when you overcome something challenging in your current life. You take your power back from this thing that was once a struggle and controlled you, and you experience the freedom of putting it behind you.

Whatever we do in one lifetime, we balance out in another. We can choose to make ourselves a better human being so that we may experience our next lifetime at a happier and more fulfilled level. Or we can choose hate and destruction and sentence ourselves to lifetimes of experiencing the same hate and destruction that we perpetrated on others. If you hate another race or people, inevitably you will be born into a lifetime as the one you hated.

*Who, then, is the true Native?* Is it the one who has lived generations experiencing the destruction of their people during the occupation, and has now returned as

White but with a red soul to help balance and heal the pain and hatred they have developed through those generations? Or is it the one who has never been Native before and is living their first Native lifetime to compensate for past racism and oppression? *The answer is neither.* They are both simply human beings who need to understand each other and heal the history of genocide that has come before them.

The indigenous way of life is based in co-existence with each other and our Mother Earth. This is in deep contrast to the colonizers who, disconnected from Earth and nature, came to new lands to take and conquer. My ancestors tell me that if the Europeans had first come to the Americas without fear and without guns and violence, we would have a much different world today than the one we all live in.

A bright light is shining in all the dark corners of our planet right now, revealing all that needs to be healed. The darkness is a disease that our earth is trying to heal from so that we all may survive. We are interconnected with her, our Mother the Earth. As we stop hurting ourselves and each other, as we heal ourselves, our Mother Earth will also heal. As we conquer fear, as we have faith, as we forgive, and as we love and heal ourselves, we become an integral part of healing our world.

My hope with this book is that my story of past lifetimes on both sides of this conflict may open your heart and mind, and allow healing to happen in whatever way is needed. I share my story because it may serve to help others understand our interconnectedness, so that we may all have compassion for each other and be able to look at each other and understand our similarities and our motivations. This understanding is what we need, so we can heal the violence currently being perpetrated on all people throughout the world, and on Mother Earth herself. By bringing love and compassion to the surface of our awareness, we heal each other and our world.

*for the good of all and harm to none*

prayers                                            2006

*My Native spirit grandfather, Onachowa, has a huge heart and big love. His name means 'the one who speaks with Spirit.' He has told me that my spirit name means the same. He then said to me, "You are the point of the arrow to pierce through the other dimensions, other worlds. You'll see these in your waking time. This is a great gift you've been given. The arrowhead is the first to pierce through the darkness."*

## when I was young

**H**ow do I remember? I have always remembered. I came into this world remembering. Now, later in my life, I understand that I have the unique gift of being able to remember my past lives or to "see through to them," you might say. I am protected, somehow, from the heavy emotions associated with these lives and I thank Creator for that. It is jarring enough to "see" and remember what happened before without having to feel deep into it now. Although, at the beginning I did feel those heavy emotions much more strongly. The strong emotional attachment at first is a part of the process, as I understand it, of integrating the significance of past life memories.

Due to my gift, I have always felt displaced. Not for lack of love — I was surrounded with love, and grateful to have a wonderful family, although I felt that the support they gave did not come from the understanding shared by my Native family. But was it still my Native family, just in a new time?

I was afraid of the dreams when I was very young. All I remembered were nightmares. I never understood them or the unsafe places, fighting, and horror they contained. I didn't like to go to bed and fall asleep, for I knew what was waiting for me. My parents did not understand what was going on. They thought I was a typical child, only artistic and overly imaginative. My sisters didn't get me at all and still struggle to understand me to this day. But how can they ever fully understand? They remember only what they experience in this life, but not past lives as well, the way that I do. It isn't their fault or mine, it's just my reality.

Sometimes, I would have a dream that wasn't a nightmare, and then it would happen in real life. I would tell my mom but she told me to keep quiet about it. Whether or not she believed me, she was afraid other people would not understand. She was trying to protect me, but at the time it made me feel very self-conscious. Now that I am more experienced in the world, I understand why she insisted I keep quiet and I'm grateful for that. My sisters never knew any of this because I kept it to myself, following my mother's wishes.

I soothed myself by drawing. I have been an artist for as long as I can remember, in all of my lives. I started painting with food coloring and paintbrushes at three. I started to oil paint at six years old. I painted constantly on whatever I could get my hands on. It brought me joy and made me feel relaxed and more confident. If I didn't have paper I used ceiling tiles, pieces of wood, rocks, anything.

My sisters would get so mad at me because I would constantly be making art. They couldn't understand why I would rather draw than play with them. It was all that I did because I felt separated from them by this secret I was keeping, and it wasn't something they wanted or were able to do. Despite the friction with my sisters, I believe my art was my saving grace and one way that my angels and guides nurtured my little soul along the way.

My mother was amazed at the things I knew how to do without being taught, like bead work. When I was seven or eight, my mother gave me a sheet and her sewing machine. I created an entire Native dress, sewing and incorporating some bead work without any instruction. My mother, God bless her, could not sew a straight line and was not able to help me much. But I had watched my Italian grandmother do a lot of sewing, so I had an idea of what to do. I cut the fringe and added beads as if I had done it before, and it felt very natural.

I spent a lot of time with my Italian grandmother at that age, and many other things began happening that I did not understand. Some Saturday evenings I would stay with them, and she and my grandfather would take me to mass. I felt safe in the extremely large Catholic church. Sometimes I would see the angels. At first I would just know that they were there, and I would look up a lot, hoping to catch a glimpse or confirmation. Sometimes I spotted a blur of white. I always knew they were smiling at me and surrounding me. I would tell my grandmother and she never believed me, of course, but I didn't know that then.

Later, at night when I was back at home and away from the safety of the angels and the church, I felt like I was being attacked. Having learned about the "Devil" through Catholic teachings at an early age, I started to associate the dark energies around me with fear, because I could not identify what or who they were and did not have any guidance to understand the "unseen world." I would wake up from a nightmare crying or screaming. The common themes of my nightmares were of battles and running for my life. Sadly, I never felt safe while sleeping, although saying my prayers before bedtime seemed to help. Then I would feel safer until I fell asleep. Now that I look back, I think I was seeing some of the same horrors that I can now remember in my waking life.

When I was spiritually mature enough to handle the information, my guides and ancestors started to communicate with me and revealed my past lives to me, one at a time. I would see these memories as if they had just happened in this life. Once I was given a memory from long ago, I would receive from the ancestors the teaching and karmic ties that this past experience was manifesting in my current life. It was a way of putting the puzzle pieces together for me. 'They' revealed to me that 'before,' when I had grown up in a tribe, my gifts were recognized at a very young age. I would have been put into training with the medicine person, or shaman as they are called now. I always had the dreams and contact with Spirit, even in these prior lifetimes. Our gifts, I was told, follow us from one lifetime to the next as we develop them. I was always an artist as well, which is why creative things were so easy for me. My soul had an interesting history, from what I understand to be true.

It seems that the age of ten was some kind of turning point for me on a psychic level. The nightmares seemed to grow stronger at that time. Soon after that started, there was a day that my parents, sisters, and I went to a country fair that we always went to every Labor Day in Connecticut. We loved it there and had so much fun. I was walking with my parents when all of a sudden I saw a man walking toward me. He was in his early twenties and had very long, black hair and was wearing a biker's black leather jacket. When I looked up and our eyes met, I remembered him! How this could be, I did not know. It was disorienting and strange. I even recognized his walk as he approached and walked by me. He was Native but had the brightest blue eyes I had ever seen, and I thought he was so beautiful. I still can't believe I had that thought at only ten years old. When I went home that day, I went into my room and started crying for my 'brother.' I didn't have a brother in this life but what I remembered was that the man with the blue eyes was my brother from another lifetime. I missed my brother and I didn't understand where these feelings were coming from. I remember after that experience actually asking my mother if I had a brother, and even asked her if I was adopted. I wrote him a card that I kept in a drawer, calling him Mark, and I never forgot him.

Later, I would find out that there was a reason for this encounter. Besides the dreams, there were a lot of inexplicable events like this that happened over the years that I would not get clarity on until I was old enough to handle the knowledge. As I grew, and the ancestors shared more snippets of past lives that explained these mysteries, I would think back to my poor, ten-year-old self who thought there was something wrong with her for having these experiences. How isolated and alone she felt because she couldn't share these experiences with others, because not only would other people not understand, but she barely understood them herself! I wish I could have comforted her in some way, but at the time there was no comfort. I had lived with a feeling of being broken.

During these same years that I was growing into my gifts, on the weekends we sometimes visited my mother's parents, whom I called Memé and Pepé. I guess we didn't go there more often because it was a little far away from our home. I loved my pepé. I would sit on his lap to watch the Red Sox play baseball, and once in a while when my mother wasn't looking, he would let me sneak a sip of his beer. He was so funny, happy, and full of life. I would follow him around in the yard and into the garden to pick fresh rhubarb to bring back to the house and eat with sugar on it. We competed to see who would make a face first when we ate a lemon. My pepé was in a band in his younger years, and when my cousins and uncles came to visit they would pull out their guitars, my pepé would get out his banjo and we would have a mini jamboree in the kitchen. This was such a happy time.

I wasn't as close to my memé, although she was loving and warm to me. She was just more reserved. I remember her sitting in her rocking chair by the window, feeding the squirrels. She was always happy to see us and would pull out the toy box from the pantry. I loved being and playing there. I found out later that there was a little rivalry between my grandmothers because my Italian grandmother wanted to have me over whenever I was free from school or other activities, and my memé didn't get to see me as often. I found this out many years later when they had both crossed over and I psychically witnessed them having the same rivalry. I laugh about it now because it serves as an example that when people cross over they sometimes still act the same way they did when they were living. I'm not sure whether this means that we always carry these aspects of our personality with us in our souls, even in spite of the wisdom that crossing over imparts, or whether the departed choose to act in this way so they can relate to us in the same way that we remember them. Whatever the case, when they come through and communicate with me in visions, it sure seems like they still behave the same way.

My memé and pepé indirectly helped me to learn the reason for other feelings I had that I could not explain. Whenever I was in the living room with my father and he would watch any television show with Native Americans in it, I would cry. I wanted to crawl into the TV and be with them. I would get so angry when one of them was hurt or mistreated. I did not know why I was feeling this hurt and anger. My memé and pepé never said anything to me about being Native American, but my mother told me and my sisters that we were. My memé was ashamed of this part of our heritage but my pepé was proud of his Native American blood. Pepé, in his later years, would tell my mother, "We are Algonquin, you know. You need to know." At the same time my memé told her to never tell anyone. I still don't know why she was so ashamed. I did not know about my pepé's feelings about his heritage until I was an adult. Later I would come to understand my connection to being part Native American, and would be grateful for my pepé's pride in passing this information on to my mother. But at the time, I just thought it was another part of us that my mother told us about, and I didn't realize the greater significance it held for me and how it tied to my feelings towards the Native people I saw on TV.

When it was time for me to enter fourth grade, I landed in an alternative, open-classroom school called Pinewood, run by a group of younger, open-minded teachers. I was there for two years, my favorite two years of school ever. Pinewood was out in the woods, so during recess we could go out and play among the trees. We had the freedom to wander around the property. I could be alone if I wanted. I would spend recesses by myself in nature, building my own fort from found branches and saplings. I built myself this small shelter and I loved it. It was my place. I didn't know at the time that part of what I loved and embraced was the sense of living in the wild. I felt safe being trusted to go into the woods because, even when alone, I knew that my friends were close by. Recess, art, and music were my favorite classes at that school. An art teacher nurtured me in the talent I had always possessed. She talked with my mom and asked if she could keep me after school to work on my art skills. I felt so special being the only one with her in the room after school. My mom still has the drawings that I made during that time, framed and up on the walls of her house. Our music instructor was a woman who played guitar and sang folk songs. I loved hearing her play that music, and loved singing along. At the end of the year there was a week where we would camp in huge army tents together, the girls in one tent and the boys in another. These days were filled with learning about nature. The lessons that stuck with me the most were those telling us what was safe to eat and what was poisonous and to be avoided. These things stuck with me in particular, because they are the things my soul remembered from times before. I flourished at that school. It was a formative period in my life.

Pinewood was an experiment and we were the first students to attend. We were only there for fourth and fifth grades. The staff was entirely focused on these grades only, so after fifth grade we had to move on and a new fourth grade class entered the school. Pinewood was only open for a few years before it was considered a success and a new, larger elementary school following the same model was built in town. The original location closed.

I felt so sad when I had to return to a regular classroom for sixth grade. It felt unfair, and I started becoming rebellious because of it. My parents thought I was just entering 'that age.' Now that I look back I realize I acted out because I was angry that my freedom to be out in nature had been taken away. School was now in a concrete building. The outdoor area for recess was covered in concrete, like a parking lot. I felt like somebody had put me in jail. I started hanging out with a girl who I knew wasn't a good influence. We would go to her house, down the street from school, and we would go up into her room to listen to Black Sabbath while her dad smoked pot in the living room. My parents soon realized I was hanging out in an unhealthy environment, and the girl's irresponsible parents were a bad influence. They quickly put a stop to me seeing her.

When I got to high school, I received a special pass that allowed me to spend study hall in the art room. Once again, the space to practice art became a sanctuary for me. Early in my junior year, in preparation for college applications, my art teacher started keeping me after school to develop a portfolio.

As I put together this portfolio for college, my psychic gifts increased and the fear and nightmares from my childhood intensified. They had never gone away, but I had become better at coping, even though I still did not fully understand. To counter my fear, I would pray to Jesus and Mary because that is what I was taught as an Italian Catholic. My Italian grandmother and Aunt had taught me how to say my prayers and do the Rosary, so I had some spiritual tools. At this age, my parents had given me my own room in the finished basement because I wanted my own space. I was struggling with issues typical of any teenager, but something more began to happen. Soon after moving into the basement room, the nightmares escalated from dreams to actual attacks.

My dad built me a loft bed for my basement bedroom, at my request. Five feet off the ground, I felt safe climbing up into it and sleeping close to the ceiling. One evening, soon after I moved into this bed, I had a nightmare that I was being attacked by a black horse with hands, hands it was using to strangle me. I woke up from a sound sleep in terror to find that I could still feel myself being strangled by what was now an unseen force. The 'horse' then yanked me from my loft bed, and as I physically fell the five feet to the floor, I screamed, "Jesus, help me!" The unseen force, or black horse, instantly vanished. I lay on the floor, breathing heavily and crying, wondering what the hell had just happened. I stayed there in shock. I don't remember what happened next or how I even coped with what transpired that night. I wouldn't learn until years later the significance of this attack and its relationship to my family history.

This attack, and others that followed, were incredibly intense. I had no idea why they were happening to me. Seeking to escape, I contemplated suicide. At this point I told my parents I wanted to die. I wanted relief! That was quite a scene. My parents asked, "How could you want to do this to us?" But I couldn't explain; I just cried and said I wanted to be with Jesus. In reality, the nightmares and attacks were so bad I couldn't handle them anymore. I know now that after my parents shared this news with my family, my Italian aunts and grandmother prayed very hard for me. Prayers are powerful. I thank my family, grandmother, and aunts for their prayers. I know they prayed for me, because my guides told me later that those prayers had a huge impact and protected me. You see, since we have free will, our angels and guides can't do anything without our asking on a daily basis. So, when I was a child and young adult, my family's prayers asked for my protection, when I didn't know how to ask it for myself.

Although I was saved from suicide by my family's prayers, I rebelled. I wore long skirts, looking like a hippie when everyone else looked preppy in high school. I started to hang around "the wall," (where the rough kids hung out) and got caught up with a tougher crowd in an attempt to cope with and escape from what was happening to me at home. My one positive outlet for this energy continued to be, my art and extra time in the art room. I am grateful to have channeled some of that energy correctly into my artwork, despite my confusion and rebellion.

In the early spring of my junior year, some friends came back from a weekend retreat, seeming to glow with joy. I asked them about it. They told me it was a Christian retreat. I looked into it and I asked my parents if I could go. Ecstatic, they jumped at the chance to bring me there. When we actually got in the car to go, I started to have second thoughts for no reason at all. Something was telling me not to go. Maybe the dark energy that was around me at this time tried to change my mind. When I told my parents I had changed my mind my mother said "too bad" and she and my father drove me there.

When we arrived, I put on my tough act. I was in a leather jacket, jeans, and my Indian shirt. I met a girl named Hannah. She dressed in preppy clothing and was initially intimidated by my persona. I laugh now because it was such a facade to help me feel safe. Hannah ended up being one of my best friends from the day we met. I am not sure if I had a healing done to me at the retreat or what, but all I know is I felt better. I felt as though I belonged and was safe, and I didn't have any nightmares while I was there. At first I thought the fact that we were sleeping in groups kept me safe, but it was really the energy of the place that deterred the nightmares. This peacefulness led me to continue going back to the retreat in other years to help other kids. Hannah and I had a lot of similar experiences while at the retreat. Once, when we were praying together in the sanctuary, we both smelled an overwhelming aroma of roses. I was later told that if you smell roses, Mary the Virgin Mother is in the room. The spiritual experiences Hannah and I shared created a very strong bond between us.

Then I met my first boyfriend, Jonah, at a rally. I walked into the gathering of hundreds of young people and I was taken aback by the level of happiness and joy in the room. The moment I entered I stopped in my track, watching the chaos of music and dancing as if time stood still. The first thing that stood out to me in the crowd was Jonah, with his long hair and beautiful smile. He looked toward me as I noticed him, and he ran up to me, took my hand, and swept me up into the energy. I didn't even hesitate to follow when he came up and took my hand, and I felt a strange whirlwind of emotions all at once.

Jonah turned out to be quite a gift to me, and made me feel safe and loved. I thought I would stay with him forever. I never told him much about my dreams. I had been keeping my mouth shut about that part of my life to everyone. I thought these abilities that I had were bad, and didn't see them as gifts. I was a typical teenager and I didn't want to be different. I wanted to fit in and be normal and have a normal life. But that was not what I got, as much as I tried to make it look that way from the outside. I tried to be like everybody else, but somehow little things always made it come out sideways that I wasn't. Those around me attributed anything unusual to my being an artist, which was safe and comprehensible for them. Yet, while I attempted to pass as normal, my angels and guides tried to teach me some tools to protect myself. I continued to do my prayers and the rosary at night. Then, the reprieve that the retreats and rally had given me ended, and I started to have even more dreams.

When the dreams resurfaced, I had been dating Jonah for five years. It was also my first year at University. Jonah had a lot of patience but I could tell I was beginning to frustrate him with my increasingly erratic behavior, which was compounded by my inability to communicate the reason for it, because I thought I had to keep the dreams a secret. More than ever, I felt uncomfortable in my own skin, and hiding things from Jonah only made this worse. The nature of the dreams had changed as well, so that not only did I feel as if I had backslid into a past from which I'd had a temporary respite, but the whole experience also felt foreign at the same time. This time the dreams were premonitory in nature, and they always came true.

Halfway through the school year, I was desperate and tired of hiding everything. I finally took a chance and confided a little of what I was experiencing with my roommate. She seemed to take my admission well and we made a game of the situation. I would dream of a scenario and the people involved. We would write it down in a notebook and see how long before it happened. This was a non-threatening game, and sharing the dreams with her helped my fear of them to dissipate. Each time we documented a dream and noted the people, the scene, and any noteworthy occurrences, we would wait expectantly to record the date when the scenario happened. They started to come true so regularly that I became overwhelmed and scared by the frequency. It stopped feeling like a game to me. Then one night I had a dream of a man I had never met. We were on a date, sitting together at a restaurant with white twinkle lights. I was alarmed that it wasn't Jonah and confused about what it could mean if I came to be on a date with someone other than Jonah. I stopped telling my roommate about the dreams, pretending they had stopped, and the game was over.

Now that the dreams seemed to be showing a future that threatened the happiness I had found, I stopped thinking clearly and wanted to escape the dreams and the future they showed. Not knowing where to turn for help, I threw myself into my work and other activities. I completed all my assignments in record time and then ran to take as many dance classes as I could. I stopped eating, and drank at parties to the point of blacking out, trying to make it all go away. Of course I just made it worse. My parents have since told me that they were so concerned when they saw how thin I had become the day they came to pick me up to go home that summer, that they almost pulled me out of school.

At that age, I did not yet know much about my Native American heritage, other than my affinity for Native people on TV. I was completely immersed in Italian Christianity. Despite the rebellious attitude I had fostered in self-defense against what I was going through spiritually, I still secretly liked going to church. Church felt safe, and there were moments when I still felt peace come over me and I would catch glimpses of the angels out of the corner of my eye. There were also moments when I was frustrated because I intuitively sensed that my soul understood explanations for what I was going through that I could not access. I didn't know how I knew this, but I was confident in it. There seemed to be some sort of block keeping information that I needed hidden inside me, and this was actually true. My guides psychically blocked this information because I was not yet mature enough to handle it. This was their way of protecting me from more than I could withstand, but it did not protect me from this uncomfortable frustration I felt. If I had known more of my Native heritage at the time, Native spiritual teachings would have helped me understand what was going on when traditional Catholicism did not. Unfortunately, I wouldn't learn this until later, and so my only real solace at the time was in my friend Hannah because of our similar mystical experiences. Although she wasn't Native, she could partially understand what I was going through. So despite how I appeared to my parents when they picked me up from school, I was relieved when it was time for summer break and I could go home and see Hannah.

Whenever Hannah and I were together, the bond between us grew. She became the closest friend I had at the time; she understood my fear and frustration because of the things we had experienced together. Smelling the roses in the sanctuary was only the first incident. Another time, we saw the white lights, or angels, during a retreat. We shared the feeling of "knowing" that we had been surrounded by Jesus, Mary, and the angels at these times. These shared experiences with Hannah made me feel less of an outcast, and I was grateful. Hannah, Jonah, and I got together a lot during that summer, but I didn't share much with Hannah in front of Jonah because I was afraid he wouldn't understand. As a result of this and the fact that we were usually all together at the same time, I didn't have Hannah's support and understanding as much as I needed. Instead of being able to confide in her over the summer, I felt isolated again, keeping these feelings and experiences to myself.

As summer progressed, Jonah seemed to be in his own world. Though I knew that I was keeping things from him, and now I can see that perhaps his distance was a response to this on some level, at the time I felt that he wasn't listening to me during even the most basic communications, and feelings of frustration began seeping into our relationship. After that tension began to grow, I left for a time to go on vacation with my family to the beach, and was away from Jonah and Hannah. Being with Jonah so much over the summer had pushed the dream of the date at the restaurant with the twinkle lights to the back of my mind, until I met the man from the dream while I was away at the beach. His name was Zac, and he asked me out right after we met. I was so startled by recognizing him from the dream that I agreed, and he took me to that very restaurant with the twinkle lights. Between feeling that Jonah was growing distant, and my sense that it must somehow be fated if I dreamt it, I broke up with Jonah later that summer after I got back from the beach.

A couple years later, before we all graduated from college, Hannah developed leukemia. I visited her whenever I could. She died around Christmas a few short years later, and it was another turning point in my life. I discovered I could hear and talk to her on the other side. After she passed, I would feel her presence when she came around me, like a subtle tingling down my spine. I would hear her tell me things, as if in a whisper. During her burial, her parents, her sister, and I hung beautiful ornaments in the tree over her grave. As we cried, Hannah blew snow over all of us with a gust of wind and we all laughed because we knew it was her. Every year for ten years after, a mass was said for her that I attended with her family. It helped us all to heal from the loss of her. But from then on, Hannah visited me and appeared in my dreams.

When someone we love crosses over, they often want to comfort those they left behind. Because of our society's limited understanding of the natural laws of the unseen world, many are afraid of this type of contact. As a result, our loved ones have to find a gentle way of reaching us and communicating what they want to say before they fully leave us. They do this by either visiting us in a dream, or by having a memory of them come into our minds. We can even sometimes "hear" them saying things they always said to us, as if remembering but with an unusual clarity and presence, reminding us of their love. These are the "safe" ways they can contact most of us, and in turn we can find comfort in that instead of fear.

Thirty years later, I was staying alone at my parents' beach cottage to do some artwork when Hannah visited me. At first she came to me during a dream in the early morning, but as I awoke, she continued to stay present with me and speak to me. She had a lot to say! She spoke of how her parents broke up after her death, and many other personal things, some that I cannot even remember. She told me that she was going to be reborn into another life and, in her way, she was saying goodbye. However, there was a part of her which I could stay connected to in spirit. The gift of spending time with her between our worlds that day was amazing. We took a long walk in a kind of surreal, spirit place I had never experienced before. Everything seemed luminescent as we walked in this landscape of greenery and nature. Colors were brighter, and there was an energy around us, almost like a bubble of light. I know she has been reborn into another life now, but I don't know where she is or if I'll ever come across her again in this life. I had a feeling I wouldn't see her again after that visit, and I am okay with that.

Over the years since these events, I have learned much about the unseen world and its natural laws. I have had many experiences, many of which were entirely supernatural. I was taught many skills and given much understanding by my ancestors, guides, and angels. No matter the subject, with education comes understanding, and then the fear of what is not understood evaporates. We are only afraid of things we do not understand. Once we learn and understand, the fear is released. This is how it was with me, and I learned that the unseen world had natural, universal laws, the same way nature does. Many people have lost the teachings of this knowledge over the years because of the Europeans' initial fears of the indigenous peoples when they first came to this (and other) continent(s). Indigenous people have a deeply rooted understanding of the unseen world and the magic that exists in life. We know that we can work with this magic when we are connected to our Source — our Creator, our angels, guides, and ancestors. There is much that all of humanity needs to learn, or, in some cases, re-learn. My ancestors have taught me that I am a 'bridge' to bring this understanding to those who need it. I can be this bridge because I was raised understanding the Christian perspective of spirituality, and was then taught the Native understanding and my connection to it. I can teach others how these spiritualities actually work together, and do not counter each other. However, there is always more to learn. As long as we recognize that we must always be learning and do not get stuck in dogmatic, stagnant ways of viewing the world, then strong prayers can transcend any barriers, whether they are based in religion, race, or our own personal beliefs and judgments. Compassion, empathy, and forgiveness are universal.

angel's wing                                    2000

*A message from Grandfather: "Experience life, don't rush through it. Your past experiences have not been bad or good, they have just been your experiences on your individual journey. This keeps you on your path to your purpose. Learn to go with the flow of life and not to force things, as if fighting a current in the river. You cannot find joy through control. You cannot find love through control. Your destiny is in the hands of Creator, and you cannot 'rush' to get there. Just trust and have faith in the flow of life, and only then will you be fulfilled by reaching your purpose."*

## a sudden loss

I t was just a typical day until the phone rang. My cousin Katherine was calling, and as I listened to her say that she had to cancel our appointment that day, I could immediately tell there was something wrong. Even though I was not alone and in my work office, I blurted, "What's wrong?!"

Time stood still. "I can't," she answered.

"You can't what?!" I demanded. "What is the matter?"

After a long silence as she gathered her strength, Katherine spoke. "They found Mick dead in his bed this morning."

I screamed "Oh my God!" as I heard her say, "I have to go."

When I hung up the phone I knew Katherine's life would never be the same, and I prayed for her in that moment as I turned around in a state of shock, scrambling to turn my focus back to work and to the person standing in my office. Right then, I suddenly and quite clearly heard Mick's voice say to me, "You think *you* are shocked? I was just as shocked!"

I hadn't seen my cousin Mick in years but I knew from the many conversations I had had with his mother that he had a girlfriend, that he lived on a farm with horses, and that he had two little boys. His loss devastated all of us. After hearing him in my office that morning, I could sense Mick around me, trying to communicate with me, but the emotions I felt in connection with his loss were temporarily blocking my ability to hear him clearly.

Even when you have psychic gifts, if something happens too close to home or to your heart, you cannot read or hear everything because your emotions block out the communication. So I called one of my dearest friends, Jayne, who is a medium. I told her about Mick, what he had said to me, and that he was trying to talk to me but I was too upset to hear him clearly. Being an objective observer, she could hear him and told me that Mick was saying: "I guess it really does matter what you eat. I had no idea." He had been eating a typical American diet of processed foods and had not been paying attention to how it was affecting his health. Mick then said, "I had a deep bruise on my leg which ended up growing a blood clot that killed me. I'm very sad, because I had reached a very sweet spot in my life with the boys and the woman that I loved." Months later when I talked to his mother, Katherine, she confirmed that he had indeed had a very bad bruise from being kicked by his horse, and was hospitalized for it because it wouldn't heal correctly.

In the days that followed the news of his death and my contact with Jayne, Mick told me it was a comfort to him that I could hear him, because he had crossed over unexpectedly and his soul was not yet ready to leave things unsaid with those he loved here on this plane. This is true with many people who cross quickly and unexpectedly. Being able to communicate with me helped Mick to say the things he needed to. I was able to tell Katherine exactly how he had passed, which at the time was still very unclear because the results from the autopsy would not be ready for months. By speaking through me, Mick was able to make it so that she did not have to wait for closure and understanding.

At the funeral, I stood in the church pew listening to Mick's brother, Paul, speak about Mick. I was blown away by the accuracy of what he said. As he talked, it was as if he was describing exactly what I had already learned through my communication with Mick. Paul described his brother crossing over to the other side and saying to everyone there, "So what is this all about?" Paul's entire account of how he envisioned his brother's passing was very intuitive and was almost exactly what happened, as told to me by Mick.

Paul is a police officer and "sees" a lot more than most people. The local and state officers that I know in my life, including my cousin and his father, have a lot of compassion but don't put up with nonsense because they use their intuition to sense when someone is not being honest. My cousin Paul is like that, and though he is not a medium or clairvoyant, this heightened intuition is how he tuned in to what his brother was experiencing on the other side and was able to accurately include it in his remembrance. Paul also spoke about the last conversation he had with his brother.

He shared that he had told Mick not to stress about the things he couldn't change and that "everything happens for a reason."

Paul then related this to the family's own experience of Mick's passing by saying, "It is true that even this happened for a reason, even though we don't know what that reason is. Only God knows." The sudden loss of Mick manifested differently in all of our lives and had different meaning for each of us. Mostly, though, his death served as a reminder to live every moment fully and appreciate what we have. I believe, as a result of the things that I have sensed, that we learn to love deeper and in a fuller way when faced with loss. We become more compassionate and more "human."

Prior to Paul's eulogy, as I had been preparing to leave for the funeral that morning, I had suddenly heard my Native spirit grandfather say, "Put your good flute in the car!"

I responded, actually out loud, talking to the air, "Why?"

He said sternly, "Just do it! Bring the one from your office, the good one."

My Native ancestry often seems to embarrass the Italian side of my family because of their lack of understanding, so I was worried about having the flute there. I put it in my car, but argued, "This is an Italian funeral."

"That's of no matter," he said. After the service, we got into our cars. I pulled into the procession line and ended up directly behind Mick's immediate family. As we drove to the cemetery, I was the last car allowed to the grave-site. I noticed all the remaining cars were directed around to the other side of the cemetery, and I thought that was odd.

"Get your flute," my grandfather said.

"Really?" I asked. I was taken back by the immediate and direct conversation I was having with him over this.

"Yes," he said. So I did what he instructed. I got out of the car and started walking up to the grave with my flute in hand, feeling very self-conscious. I noticed that nobody else had gotten out of their cars yet, so I turned to go back. My intention was to put my flute back, but Grandfather told me no.

"Open up your coat," he said to me, "and put it underneath. If you feel the moment is right, then you will play. If you do not feel right or comfortable, then you don't have to."

This made me feel better since I wouldn't have to have it out in the open, or be forced to play. After the burial service, they made an announcement that we could get back into our cars. I was standing behind Katherine when she turned around for a moment and locked eyes with me. I discreetly pulled out the flute and asked her if she wanted me to play.

She quickly looked around and asked, "Is the priest gone? Only if the priest is gone."

"Playing the flute isn't religious," I mouthed, expressing my confusion on my face.

I couldn't see why playing a flute would matter to the priest, but recognized that this was that "Italian perception" I was concerned about. Deep down I knew I'd send prayers along with the music, but I kept that to myself.

In that quick moment, she surveyed the immediate area and said, "The priest is gone... Okay."

So I walked to the head of the casket. Mick's girlfriend was laying a white rose and saying her goodbyes, and I started to play as she finished. Everyone stopped talking and listened. I played the prayer song that my ancestors had taught me to use for healing, knowing that most of those who were listening had no idea this was its purpose. It was still soothing in the moment, and when I was done, Mick's girlfriend looked up at me and thanked me. It felt very right to have played, and I had an overwhelming sense that Mick had wanted me to. I hugged Katherine and her husband, James, who also thanked me.

As I went to leave, I was stopped by another sensation from Mick. Mick's girlfriend came around from the other side of the grave. In that instant I heard Mick ask me to pass a message to her, and so I grabbed her hands. I looked up at her and introduced myself saying, "I am Mick's cousin. He wants you to know that when your baby smiles, you will know he's standing there." She smiled at me in gratitude and I told her to contact me if she needed anything.

As I walked away, I was shaking, for I had never been so intensely instructed in the moment. I was hoping I did the right thing when I heard Grandfather say lovingly, "Yes, you did."

One evening many weeks later, I heard from Katherine. We talked for quite a while, as I shared with her what her son was channeling to me and wanted her to know. She was so grateful because it eased her soul to know the truth, and the additional details that I could share about his death. As we were finishing our conversation, I said to her, "He is saying when you see the Christmas lights blinking, it's him."

She was immediately shocked. For two weeks the white Christmas lights on the tree in the yard outside their house had been blinking, and her husband, James, was trying to figure out why, because Katherine dislikes blinking lights. They had taken them down, thinking there was a short in the wire. In reality, it was her son letting her know he was there. She said to me, "You didn't know that!"

I replied, "No I didn't, but Mick did." In that very moment I heard him laughing.

Mick's death and its lesson for me, to remember how unexpectedly life can be taken away, are the reasons I'm writing this book now. My ancestors have been telling me for a while that they wanted me to write my story. I've told them that I am not a writer, I am an artist. They said I may not be a "writer" but I will be an author and a storyteller.

Mick's death was a catalyst and helped me to see that I want to do something really good in the world before I go on. I am being nudged by Spirit to move forward into the unknown, and I am no longer afraid of what others think of me. I am here for a purpose, and I will do what I must. I'm also here to heal what has been done to my family and my lineage from this life and from many lives before.

day to night                          2006

*"No hay mal que por bien no venga." Meaning: "There is no bad that does not bring some good with it." Abrazo and Light, Juanita*

# the black horse

It took many years before I was given any clarity on the attack I experienced as a teenager while asleep in my loft bed, though the incident left me forever changed. The unseen force that came through in my dream as a black horse had already been there, building in strength unbeknownst to my family, or even to me, until the night of the attack. My feelings of wanting to commit suicide were really manifesting from my desire to escape from that dark energy present in the house. I was the only one affected this way, because it was focused on me. At age fifteen, I didn't understand what was happening, and I couldn't explain what I *did* know to my parents. I was so afraid and felt I had no one to turn to. It seemed I was the only one being attacked, so I moved out as soon as I was able.

We were always told that my memé's mother had taken her own life. Her three children, my memé included, were all thrown into an orphanage afterwards by their father, who did not care to raise children on his own. Memé's older brother was able to leave the orphanage after a few years because of his age. Her younger sister was adopted and had a decent life. But my Memé was not so lucky. She grew up in foster homes, and I've only heard stories of a few of the horrible things she endured. In one home she was treated as a slave, having to do all the cooking and cleaning. One day she was lifting up a boiling pot of water and she dropped it and was severely burned. She was too young to be doing that kind of work. I can only imagine what other abuses she endured at such a young age. She was shuffled from foster home to foster home until she was old enough to get out of the system. She always felt that her mother had abandoned her, but this was not the reality. Many years after the attack of the black horse, when I could hear Spirit clearly, my great-grandmother came to me in spirit so that I could share with the family the truth of what happened.

I went to visit my mother one afternoon, and we were discussing some unexplained occurrences that were happening around the house. There was an uneasy feeling in the atmosphere. A close family member, Anne, and her children had been staying there a short period of time, and one night she felt something, an energy or dark shape, hovering over her two year old baby in the crib. The energy was so strong that even Anne, who was not sensitive to the supernatural, was aware of it, and then the baby started to scream inconsolably. This was the start of a new and disturbing pattern that continued on for many nights. My mother was concerned, and we were trying to make sense of what was happening. We got on the topic of our Native lineage, because I was doing research into our genealogy at the time. My mom had recently received some photos of my great-grandmother and other family members, and we started looking through them. We began discussing the story we had always been told, of how my memé had been put into the orphanage after her mother's suicide. Moments later, I left my mom and walked down the hallway to retrieve something from the bedroom, when I suddenly heard the following in a shockingly forceful and angry tone.

"I DID NOT COMMIT SUICIDE! I would NEVER have left my children to that monster!"

At this time my psychic perception was still sporadic, and I didn't understand it fully yet, so it startled me enough to start my heart racing. But I knew immediately it was my great-grandmother.

"He murdered me because I was Native and strong-willed!" I heard her continue. I knew she must mean her husband who was French-Canadian. "He poisoned me right in front of my children! I would never have abandoned my children with that monster! You tell the family the truth!" I ran back to the kitchen, shaking, to tell my mother what had just happened.

In the days and years to follow, as my abilities got stronger, I learned that by revealing the truth and clearing my great-grandmother's name, a healing could begin for all of the women in the family who had been abused. I was told by my guides that the abuse kept rearing its ugly head again and again in our family so that we could eventually conquer it and heal our lineage. They said that when you heal a particular abuse in your own life, it causes a ripple effect for those who came before you and for those who come after you. That particular negative pattern's lesson can then be learned by all involved and will no longer need to be experienced. Once I, or any person, overcomes or heals a trauma or negative pattern in my own life, it clears on all levels: physical, emotional, and spiritual. In being cleared from all levels of our Being at once, it can then be released. This release allows for the soul to be healed, and that healing then releases those who are yet to come in future generations from the karmic ties that perpetuated the abuse. In Native ceremony it's common to pray for seven generations yet to come, for the spiritual and physical well-being of the family. But now from the teachings I have received from my ancestors, I understand that this healing propels back seven generations as well.

When my great-grandfather died, my memé received a call from the lawyer handling his death and estate, who had somehow tracked her down after all those years. She had never seen her father again after he put her and her siblings in the orphanage. The lawyer called her to have her "collect his things." There wasn't much; a watch, a lamp, and a few other small items. She didn't want any of it, but picked them up and put them away in her house. Years later, when my memé and pepé passed away and the family cleaned out the house, the watch and lamp went to my mother and then came to reside in our house. That's exactly when the attacks began happening to me. When I was fifteen. It was my memé's father. He had followed his items into the house, and appeared as the black horse that attacked me.

After the terrifying night of that first attack, the black horse would come back many times. I have vivid recollections of those nights when the black horse was present. It didn't happen every night, but when it did, I lay there in complete fear. I would all of a sudden 'feel' a presence next to me in my bed, and a wave of terror would come over me. I would pull the blankets over my head and my heart would race. I would tell myself, *"There is nothing there. What are you afraid of? To be alone in the dark?"* But when I felt this presence, I could not shake the fear. I would immediately grab the rosary beads I kept next to my bed and pray until I could finally fall asleep.

From what I have learned, a soul that chooses not to go into the light when they cross over can sometimes get stuck in the "in-between" place, which is a lower astral realm. They can be so obsessed with not leaving this life that they resist and can attach to material things, even things that they owned. My French-Canadian great-grandfather's spirit had attached to his things and come into my family's home when they were brought in. Abusive in life, to my great-grandmother and their children, he remained abusive in death. As soon as he was in the house and sensed a vulnerable presence, my presence, he began physically attacking me.

In that small basement bedroom I faced this dark energy, but I did not know how to fight it. He did a lot of damage to my self-esteem, whispering vulgar comments to me continuously and encouraging me to kill myself. He was mentally abusing me from the other side, and I did not know that these thoughts and interactions were coming from the same dark energy that physically pulled me from bed. I wasn't able to tell my parents about these details because I didn't even understand them fully myself, but this was why I wanted to die and be with Jesus. This was why I was suicidal. I'm so glad my angels and guides protected me from that. Part of my choosing to go to a college far from home was to get away from the house and get away from *him*. I knew I needed to leave to escape the torment that I was experiencing. I did return occasionally, moving in and out of my parents' home throughout my younger years as many young people do, as I transitioned between school terms, new jobs, and the like. When I lived away from their house I never experienced the "attacks," and I did not make the connection that they only happened when I returned home. The timing of my visits home, and the subsequent attacks, were so sporadic that I did not put two and two together. Each time I came back, though, the abuse would start to happen again until I would finally struggle to find a way to move out. Though it seems obvious now, I was not conscious of this pattern then. When I finally moved out for good, he must have started amusing himself in other ways. My parents started to sense a presence themselves, and actually started to witness occurrences in the house.

It was twenty years after my final encounter with the black horse when Anne sensed the dark energy over her baby's crib while she stayed in my parents' house. She had been staying there with her two daughters for a short period of time, to escape an abusive relationship. On the numerous evenings that she would see or feel the dark energy, the girls would cry. Traumatized, Anne called me to tell me what she was seeing and feeling in the middle of the night. It didn't make any sense to her. During those nights, the girls' crying also woke my parents. We all became very concerned. We knew something had to be done. I told my family to have a Catholic priest come and bless the house. I thought this would be enough to remove the bad force. When they followed my advice, the priest told them that he felt this was a bigger problem and that we needed someone stronger, who understood this "type of thing." The priest's assessment terrified everyone even more.

One evening shortly after the priest's visit, the youngest of the two girls told Anne that her "brother Nacoma" was in the room playing with her. She giggled and laughed, pointing with her finger, then said, "Look, an owl! There he goes." Her finger followed his "flight" across the room. My parents were shocked. I was relieved, because I knew this was a sign that she was being protected by Spirit from what was in the house. Children, between the ages of one month to five years old, have the ability to "see" the unseen world. For most, this ability is lost by the time they are about six years old. I'm not sure why all children have this ability only for most of them to lose it, or why it occurs on this time-line, but it explains many strange imaginings that kids can have.

Another evening, following the "appearance" of Nacoma, the family was having dinner when the youngest girl looked up to the ceiling and said, quite matter-of-factly, "Look! Jesus' daddy. How 'bout that?" She then went on eating her dinner as if nothing spectacular had happened. I wasn't there for either of these instances, but when my mother told me of them I was relieved to know that, even if there was dark energy in the house, there was obviously protection as well. Very good protection if "Jesus' Daddy" was showing himself to the little one!

At this time I was in the midst of slowly being introduced to Native American spiritual ways, and attended Pow Wows and other Native gatherings. Through this process I had recently met a local Abenaki man, and learned that he could clear energies from a home or other physical spaces. I called and told him of the occurrences, and the fact that they had not been stopped after the priest's blessing. I asked if he could help, and if he would be willing to come to my parents' home. He agreed to help and came to the house one afternoon a few days later. I was at work, so Anne let him in the house and showed him where the frightening occurrences had taken place. After going through the home and performing a cleansing ceremony, which included smudging the entire home with the smoke of burning desert sage, he said, "I've done what I can and it will be OK for a few days, but there is something very strong in the house and this will not keep it away for good."

The Abenaki man then gave us the name of a local minister who worked with deeper, stronger energies and had some success in clearing them. A few weeks later, this minister came to the house. After a thorough walk-through, she sat us down and told us, "This is more serious than I can handle, but don't worry. I know someone who can." She referred us to this person: Jayne Gabrielle.

While all of this was happening, I had gained some memories of my past lives, but I did not understand them for what they were, nor what their context was in this life. I had repressed a lot of my memories and abilities so I could function in society. Everybody's gifts are different. Now that I understand mine, I would never label myself a medium or psychic. Although I can hear quite clearly when my ancestors have something to tell me, and I can understand who the message is coming from, that does not seem to be where my strengths are. Jayne, however, is a medium, a psychic, and a healer. I believe her presence in my life is a gift given to me by God. What I knew then was just the tip of the iceberg; her knowledge was like the rest of the iceberg hidden beneath the surface of the water. At this critical point, I desperately needed help, and Jayne became my friend, teacher, and healer from then on.

The day Jayne arrived at my parents' home, I answered the door and immediately felt a sense of relief. When I first met her, I knew that we had a connection. I heard a voice tell me, "She will become a long-time friend." I also had an overwhelming sense of recognition the moment she walked through the door. Jayne entered my life at exactly the right moment. I had reached a point in my psychic development where I could start to wrap my mind around what had happened to me and what was happening in my parents' house, so I was able to witness what Jayne could do and understand it. Though I now understand the timing of this meeting in relation to my psychic development, at the time I did not realize how much Jayne would teach me. Though I had not yet come to understand my past life memories, I had learned many Native ways from a couple of Native teachers. I was hearing my spirit grandfather clearly on occasion, but not consistently. With these learnings and advancements I was feeling a lot more confident in my gifts, and thought that I had learned quite a bit about them. Meeting Jayne changed everything for me. I thought I knew a lot about the unseen world, but after meeting Jayne my ego was put in check, and I realized I knew nothing in comparison to her. As my relationship with her has progressed, I have learned that there is always someone ahead of you on your personal journey from whom you can learn, and there is also always someone behind you whom you can teach. Now, after years of knowing each other and growing together in our knowledge, I know that Jayne and I arranged this meeting before either of us came down into this life. I have a feeling that I refused to "come back" without her, and our angels and guides arranged it.

Jayne walked through the door that day with such confidence, assessing the events we'd experienced. I followed her instructions without question because I was "tuned in" to her and felt from Spirit that everything she said was right. She told us the process would take a number of days and require some difficult work on my part because I played a huge role in how the situation came to be. After she visited a couple times, Jayne was able to help us understand the entire story behind the situation. As a skilled medium she interpreted all that had happened, and explained it to us. As she helped us all to understand what we were facing, she told me, "You're a critical part of clearing this energy."

The reason, as she explained it, turned out to be related to one of the few keepsakes I had of my great-grandmother: a single photo of her. When I was younger, I didn't look much like anyone in my family. I had dark hair while my sisters were both blonde, like my mom. My dad, being Italian, is dark-haired. I do look a bit like my dad, but my features are different. I never really knew where my features came from until I found this photo of my great-grandmother. She is who I look like. Jayne explained that this is why my great-grandfather targeted me. I was a familiar outlet for his anger and abuse. He recognized that I had the same gifts that my great-grandmother did. He recognized that not only did I look Native, but my soul was Native too. He knew these truths before I learned them. As Jayne explained why my great-grandfather singled me out, I listened and worked with her because I wanted the abuse to finally end. I saw her as my only hope. Because Jayne had been able to see the whole story, she knew how to proceed where others could not. She told us, "His energy is too strong in the home. He has been here a long time. We will need to do a ceremony in the back yard and call him out of the house."

It took me a while to prepare for the ceremony. First, we removed from the home any items that came from my great-grandfather, as Jayne instructed. She told me to take the last item, my great-grandfather's watch, and bury it in the earth when I was alone. On the day I went outside to do this, I could suddenly feel him standing behind me as I walked into the yard. I stopped and turned to face him. Instead of the fear I had felt all those years, I felt strength in knowing that there was something I could do to help myself, and that I was doing it, with Jayne's help. Although I could not see him, I sensed his extreme anger towards me. I didn't care. I had had enough of his abuse, and I told him so out loud. Turning, I began walking again to complete the task of burying the watch. After a few steps I felt his energy move before me, stabbing me in the center of my chest. I didn't stop, and kept walking forward, through his energy, and buried the watch without further incident. I immediately called Jayne and told her what had happened. After a few minutes of silence, she explained: "He hit you with a 'psychic arrow' and it backfired on him. Instead of hurting you, he basically gave you what is equal to an inoculation. He can now no longer hurt you the way he did before. You have taken some of your own power back from him." In that moment, I felt a huge sense of relief.

When the day came for the final ceremony, Jayne had a friend, Gary, come to join us for it, in order to "hold the energy." She said we needed the power of another person in the ceremony, because my family members would watch but not partici-pate. My mom was understandably a bit self-conscious about us doing this ceremony out in the back yard in broad daylight, but we had no choice, and now that she understood, she wanted my great-grandfather's hold over the family and house to be over as well. When my family and I went out to the backyard there was a palpable feeling of anticipation, but mixed with fear because we were all Catholic and this sort of ceremony was foreign to us. As I sat with Jayne and Gary, I felt butterflies in my stomach but I was ready.

The first thing Jayne did was to command my great-grandfather's ghost to come out of the house to where we were. I was shocked when I felt his presence immediately. Jayne was quiet for a moment and then told us that an amazing thing had happened. Mother Mary was there, and in that instant I felt her incredible presence. I knew that she had come because of all the years I had said the rosary and asked for protection. I felt surrounded with love, and a great sense of compassion came over me. As this feeling engulfed me, I began to speak directly to my great-grandfather.

The first thing that came out of my mouth was, "I forgive you." I hadn't planned on saying that, and I felt his immediate shock, as that was the last thing he had expected to hear from me.

"You are still a member of my family," I continued, "and even after all you have done, I still love you and I forgive you." I continued to feel his surprise at these words, and felt his energy shift. I don't even know where my words came from, but it was as if my great-grandmother spoke through me. I felt her presence with us.

"Wow," Jayne began to speak, explaining what was happening because we couldn't see it. "I've never seen this before. His soul has split in two! One part light and one dark! The dark part of him will stayed buried in the earth with his watch for now, to stay with the earth to heal. Mother Mary took the part of him that was light with her. He will now have to deal with the healing of his karma, and this will have to play out. He will have many lifetimes struggling with a feeling of not being 'whole,' until his soul has healed and the parts are reunited. He will need your prayers."

On hearing this, I thought, "Ok, now it is up to God."

When the ceremony was complete, we all just sat looking at each other for a few moments. Jayne lay down on the grass, and my parents went into the house where they had a meal prepared for us. As we followed them in, I felt an overwhelming sense of gratitude and relief and a great shift in the energy in and around the house.

Fifteen years after clearing the house of the black horse, I was looking at my great-grandmother's photo when I heard her say to me, "Take that photo of me and get me out of those European peoples' clothes. Put me in my traditional Native clothing." I have started to repaint this picture of her so that she is wearing traditional Native clothing. A few weeks ago, a salesman I never met before came into my office. Our meeting got interrupted for a moment, and while he waited for me, he saw the photo of my great-grandmother on my shelf. When we resumed our conversation he looked at me and said, "Is that you? It looks just like you." I said, "No, that's my great-grandmother." I have had many people ask me that same question when seeing her photo since then. I am very proud to look like her, and I am grateful that I was able to help clear her name. Now, with full understanding, I have been able to close a terrifying chapter of my life and help the entire family heal and move forward.

spirit guides                                    2005

*I am the seventh generation that my grandfather prayed for. He prayed our ways would not be forgotten and that his children's children, to seven generations, would one day remember who they were.*

# ancestry

Recently, I traveled up to Canada for the fast and sweats that we hold for preparation prior to ceremony. On the last morning of the fast, I was startled awake upon hearing a woman's evil laugh. Instead of fearing it, I took a deep breath and asked my ancestors what this was about. "*Who was she?*"

"She is the last living relative of your step-grandsons," they answered. "She was abused in the residential schools and her mind is not healthy. Do not research their genealogy any further until she makes her spirit journey, and we will tell you when to continue."

My grandfather then said to me, "Just as you will, of course, protect your grandsons because you love them and do not want them to be harmed, so too is the reason why you were born into an Italian, white family at this time. So you could be protected from harm as well." I started to cry with this realization.

I did not grow up on a reserve, and over the years I have struggled with the issue of identity. My soul's memories are real, as if the struggles I endured in past lives happened in real time to me in this life. But those memories are not from this life. In this life, I was born into a safe environment in order to allow my soul to recover from the intensities of the last few lives I lived. I struggle with this because I can identify so closely with all those who have grown up on reserves in this life and continue to struggle under the aftermath of colonialism, but if they do not believe me or under-stand the ways of Spirit, they think my understanding of them is not legitimate. I have a connection to my Native ancestral bloodline in this lifetime, but that is only part of who I am genetically and spiritually. I didn't even know what that meant until halfway through my life. My ancestors have told me, "Be authentic. The truth of who you are will be revealed when your soul finally meets its purpose." I have a small part in healing the whole, and for that I am responsible.

I do not need to focus on who believes my experience and who does not. Yet it is difficult to feel that I am being authentic and doing my part when people think that I am using stories and history that, to them, do not look as though they belong to me because of my genetic identities in this lifetime. Though I try to take comfort in my ancestors' words to get over this feeling, it is still a struggle. This is true for all people, not just myself. Whether you can trace your ancestors' blood lineage directly to the blood running through your veins, or whether you only feel the connection through your soul, you're still here to heal our Mother Earth and to heal past traumas to "your" family line. The issue of cultural identity, and how we identify ourselves individually, is important only to us personally. Prejudice and racism are the effects of people focusing too much on their current identity and how it differs from others, rather than focusing on what we all have in common and what we can do to help each other heal and progress.

Grandfather explained judgment to me. He said, "Imagine you are looking at the outline of a human being. Then envision that human surrounded in light that includes a spectrum of all colors. Now, as you stand next to them, you fixate on the color blue, to the point where you only see the color blue and none of the other colors. When only fixated on one color, you do not see the entire human being, only that one aspect or trait. That is what judgment is."

It is hard to overcome this view, however, because the pain and trauma caused by racism and prejudice are very real. Here in the Northeast, we now struggle to recover cultures and ancestries that were destroyed or hidden by genocide and assimilation from the first part of the American colonization. From my memories of my past lives, I recall these words that were said by the elders to the white soldiers who were involved in the massacres during the westward expansion: "We will be born again and return as your sons and daughters." From what I have been told by my ancestors, this has come to pass as a way to help create the needed empathy between the souls that have had either a European or Native history.

Even though I sometimes struggle to balance my current life and past life memories, one thing I know for sure is that my connection to my ancestors is strong. They continue to guide and teach me every day. My spirit grandfather, Onachowa, was Blackfoot. His ways were, and still are, powerful, and he has strong medicine. When he prays, I can feel his strength and this gives me faith in his guidance through all that I do. My family's connection to our Native lineage was broken when my great-grandmother was murdered. Other families lost their connection through adoption, children taken to residential schools, or displacement of family members who pursued work or other necessities. After my great-grandmother's murder, the rest of my family hid that part of their identity to protect their children from the prejudice and stigma that indigenous people had to endure. Many Native families were just trying to survive and protect their children by having them blend in and not be seen as Native. Though my family recognized the importance of telling us that we were Native, nothing more was said about it after that. We lived in a world that did not see Native people as equals. As a result, the connection to our traditions was cut, and I would have a long road ahead to reconnect with and heal my family's lineage.

When I was searching for my memé's Native lineage about twenty years ago, going from reserve to reserve on the East coast of Canada, I was guided by my ancestors to places all across the Gaspé Peninsula. I found my pepé's name, along with the names of his father and brothers, in the Malecite tribal rolls in Canada. Finding this information was difficult at the time, because tribes were receiving some government benefits, and suddenly opportunists who had heard a story of a Native in their family were out to prove their heritage to get those benefits, even though neither they nor their families had ever lived on or been close to a reserve. This was not my intent. My ancestors started waking me in the middle of the night to tell me I needed to find this information, which shocked and scared me. I had not grown up in the environment of the Native reserves, and had no idea what was ahead of me. But once I started the search, it was hard to convince anyone of my true motives. When I found my pepé's name and family, I told the woman in charge of the rolls. She immediately closed the book and made me leave. She had just been humoring me and hadn't really expected me to find my family, but when I did, she did not want me to make the final connection of proof. After that, I was never able to contact her again. At first I was upset at her reaction, but I understood the threat that was posed to limited tribal resources by all of these distant connections coming out of the woodwork for a share. It was enough for me to have found them and know that what my pepé had told me was true. I was given this small glimpse of the truth so that I could move forward to relink my family to who we are and where we came from. Since then, I have found that we are Blackfoot, Mi'Kmaq, and Malecite (Algonquin). I was guided to these discoveries through the story of my family's migration, as told to me in spirit by my Native grandfather.

My grandfather's people came from Northwest of the Great Lakes region. He was Blackfoot and only a young man at the time the Europeans started coming to our continent in droves. When they began arriving, the tribe decided to move westward to get away from the Europeans. My grandfather and a few other young men decided that they wanted to go East instead, and went in the opposite direction from the tribe. They traveled far along the St. Lawrence, and eventually my grandfather met and married my grandmother. Her people were Mi'Kmaq and lived on the Gaspé in Quebec, Canada. He never saw his Blackfoot family again. I am his seventh generation granddaughter, and he has told me that I am to bring our ways back to my family to heal our lineage and reconnect with the family that was lost so long ago.

At the same time that I first started learning about my deep connection to my lineage, I also learned that I was never alone. My angels and guides have been with me, protecting and guiding me, for my entire life. But now I was starting to meet more of my spirit guides on a more frequent basis. They were introducing themselves to me, now that I was speaking with Grandfather and I knew that they were there. One night I dreamt that I was in a barren room of boards, like a shack, and I sat across a table from this beautiful, black–skinned woman who was very dear to me. I was very upset. I pointed to my skin, saying to her, "Look at this! Look how light my skin is!" I was yelling at her with tears in my eyes, saying, "I do not want to be this color. Why am I? I want my skin dark!"

The woman started to laugh, a very deep belly laugh, and then said to me, "Honey, you had to be this color in this life. It is part of your purpose. It is part of your karma, for you hated the white people in many lifetimes. So now, in this lifetime, you have to experience being white. You are a bridge for the healing." She said this matter-of-factly and continued to laugh as I woke from the dream.

In the dream, the woman's wisdom had seemed to fill the space we shared as I intently listened to her, thrilled that she was visiting me. Upon waking, I could still feel her immense love for me, and I felt an amazing connection with her. The lessons you learn through each of the lifetimes that you endure stay with your soul forever. You may not have an actual memory of them, but they become innate to who you are and who you will become. None of this experience is ever wasted, not even a single lesson you learn or a single talent you develop along the way.

I tell my nieces, nephews, and grandchildren that we all have a treasure inside of us. Nobody else can tell us where or what it is. We have to find it ourselves by going within, by truly getting to know ourselves. Once we do, that gift will be revealed to us. Creator has given each of us a purpose for being here, and we have only to seek it out within ourselves. To know yourself is to know your connection with the divine, and your purpose. This can only become clear when you mature and grow, physically, mentally, and spiritually. Once you are ready, synchronicities happen in your life that you cannot explain, but they serve as validation that you are moving in the right direction and fulfilling your purpose. These events not only validate your path forward, but also make the path easier for you. Once this process begins, do not let fear get in your way. Have courage, patience, and compassion. Be fearless in faith, and you will accomplish what your soul has come here to do.

In order to reach that place of forward motion, we need to take responsibility for ourselves on an individual basis first. As we do that, we can then heal ourselves, our loved ones, our families, our people, and our ancestors. The ripple effect will continue out through the generations endlessly. We are each put on this planet with a unique gift from Creator. It is up to each of us to find that treasure inside ourselves and offer it in service to others, as we strive to be better "human beings." If we are successful in finding this purpose, we can have an impact that is not only apparent to those lives we touch now, but echoes throughout generations.

merging of the warrior and warrioress                    1998

*The ancestors say to me: "You must find compassion and forgiveness for others and yourself. As you find forgiveness for yourself, it will emerge for others."*

# soul contracts

There are moments in life when the veil between worlds becomes thin. Dealing with grief and loss can either bring about those moments, or be an example of them. The memories and feelings of certain events that happened many years ago in this life were buried as deep as I could bury them, but they held as much, if not more, power as any of my past life memories. For me to move forward into the next phase of this life, they could not stay buried.

I came home late from my office one night feeling as if something was not right. As I sat down on the couch and checked the time, I heard Zac say to me, "I'm standing here with our son." I was completely startled, hearing only his voice, but I knew instantly what it must mean.

I cried out, "What? Oh my God! You died!" I picked up the phone and called my friend Luke, who confirmed that Zac had passed away an hour before. As shocked as I was by the news of his death, I was just as shaken by what he had said about being with the son we had conceived but never had. I had made that choice, and carried the guilt of it with me for my entire life.

Zac and I had spent every moment we could together the summer before my sophomore year at University. I also met my dear friends Ellen and Luke that summer. Luke was already Zac's best friend, and that's how we were introduced. At the time I was young and naïve and oblivious to a lot that was going on around me. Zac's family liked me immediately, which made me happy because we shared our Italian heritage and its focus on the importance of family. What I didn't know was that Zac was a cocaine dealer and addicted as well. I had never touched drugs, and still refused to even after I eventually discovered that he was a dealer. He was impressed by my resolve, maybe in part because it meant I had something in common with his best friend. Luke was not involved in the drug scene the way Zac was, and therefore was one of the few people he could trust completely. Maybe the fact that I wished to remain out of it too served as the foundation for trusting me as well. He liked that I was with him for who he was and not for what he did, or for the access to drugs it could have provided. Zac's face would light up whenever I was around, and his friends and family would tell me that they could easily see how happy I made him. Zac always respected my refusal to be involved with drugs, and he kept me from that environment as much as he could, which I took as him showing how much he cared for me. Zac's protectiveness allowed me to forgive his own involvement.

All that summer, Zac wined and dined me. He took me backstage at outdoor concerts. We spent time in nature and went camping. After I finally had to go back to school, Zac rented a Lincoln and brought Ellen and Luke out to visit me, and we all went to Niagara Falls. I was so happy that he made such an effort to see me, even when we were farther apart.

Only a little while after that fall visit, I found out I was pregnant. I confided everything in my roommate, both the pregnancy and Zac's work and background. She bluntly asked me what the hell I thought I was doing. Her response was a reality check for me. I realized that I was not mature enough to have a baby. This realization brought with it a barrage of decisions that would affect me for the rest of my life. The possible arrival of a baby brought clarity to me about my relationship with Zac. I knew I would not bring a child into an environment of drugs and dealing, and something very deep inside of me was adamant about that. Once I had made that decision I was too distraught to think straight, and my roommate arranged everything for me. I called Zac and told him about the pregnancy, and that I was having an abortion and needed money sent right away. He was upset and did not want me to have the abortion, but he knew there was no changing my mind after that call.

After that, I couldn't talk to anyone else. I walked around unconsciously holding my stomach. I didn't even know I was doing it. When the appointment time arrived, my roommate's boyfriend drove me to the clinic and then it was done. When it was over, the doctor asked me if I wanted to know the sex of the baby. After a few moments of hesitation, I nodded my head yes. I was told it was a boy. I was so numb

I couldn't even comprehend what I had just done. I finally built up the courage to visit our college's priest for confession. I still remember leaving his chambers. I had been so distraught, but in that moment experienced a brief sense of calm when he lovingly told me I was forgiven. I felt that this priest had true compassion for me. But even with his blessing I could not accept that I was forgiven. The guilt plagued me for a long time.

After I began to recover from the procedure, my roommate persuaded me to face what Zac was. It was abundantly clear to her that I shouldn't date someone so involved with drugs, but all I could focus on were the feelings I had for him. Beyond being in love, I felt that my soul had known him before and that he was special to me. As I would learn later, this was true, and my feelings were so strong because they were linked to our karmic ties. Still, after my roommate's prompting, I decided to write him a letter, asking him to give up the drugs for me. I truly thought in my heart that he would, of course, give them up for me. He loved me. I was not at all prepared for what happened next.

Zac was furious when he received the letter. He called me and asked me if I meant what I said in that letter, and I said I did. I stated the ultimatum again, "Me or the drugs?" I still thought he would choose me until he slammed down the phone and hung up on me. I was shocked. I called back and he did not pick up again. That was his answer. The addiction had him and it was stronger than our love.

I could never have prepared myself for that reaction, and in that moment I felt like something broke inside my soul. I ran outside into the dark and collapsed in the road, crying hysterically. No one else was around that night, so no one came out to console me. I stayed there for a long time and cried and cried from a place deep inside me that I did not fully understand. I cried like that until I couldn't cry anymore. In that moment of slamming down the phone, Zac had made a devastating choice for both of us, and had broken his "soul contract" with me.

After that night, Zac carried on with the life to which he had committed himself, and I moved on with mine. A few months later, I got a call from Ellen, who was crying. She told me that Zac had had an accident. He had been on a ladder while working and fallen off. Zac was paralyzed from the neck down. His friends and family had a benefit for him a few months later. The news was so devastating that, despite how painful the breakup had been, I went to show my support and see Zac. When I walked up to him in that wheelchair, our eyes met and I felt only love coming from him. We were both full of emotion as the tears welled up in our eyes, and I hugged and kissed him. Shortly after I arrived, one of his sisters came up to me. She said to me with tears in her eyes, "Had my brother picked you, this never would have happened to him." I knew she was right, and I knew that Zac knew it too.

---

In the years since, whenever I have to face anything in my life that has to do with any type of endurance or courage, I think about Zac and it gets me through whatever I am coming up against. For the thirty years he spent paralyzed in bed, Zac never complained. I still think about all the lives he touched and the people he helped in spite of his early lifestyle and later limitations. I think about how a child once conceived, whether ultimately born into this world or not, links our souls together. Zac and I kept that secret from everyone for those thirty years. We cried about our choice and our loss. He shared how furious he was at me for making that life-altering decision without his consent, and I made him see how at the time I saw no other way out. Deep down I knew something was wrong. I knew that he would make the choice he did, and therefore I felt that I couldn't justify bringing a child into that world. Yet, even after we shared our mutual grief together, I never forgave myself for that choice, and I never had children after that.

Once we were able to put the hurt behind us, Zac and I stayed friends and had a deep connection that nobody else understood. For him, he was grieving the loss of a single child. For me, I felt the pain of that loss compounded by the pain from the loss of many children from different past lives. Because this pain was so great, I chose to throw myself into a career and a life without children. I chose freedom from a man I loved, rather than allowing his choices to control mine. Yet, whether we chose to be together or not, our karmic ties meant we had lessons we were destined to learn from one another. So even though we went our separate ways from the relationship, it was this deep connection that allowed us to heal enough from our choices to maintain our friendship and forgive each other.

This is why the shock of hearing his voice, and of hearing that he was with our son, made his loss almost as devastating as if we had still been together. It was also why I attended his services, despite knowing how hard it would be for me. His wake was an intense mixture of characters: from loving family and friends, to bikers from a local motorcycle club. Zac had hosted many benefits over the years, raising money for anyone struggling, so during the wake the line of people there to show his family their support stretched out the door. There was a slide show playing across the room from his coffin, commemorating him with images from life. When I walked up to watch it, I was shocked to see many photos of him and I in our younger years. His sister appeared next to me while I watched, and said, "I hope you don't mind, but those photos of the two of you together were the happiest days of his life. I had to include them." She continued, telling me that he had insisted my artwork always be placed around him, even until the week he died.

At the funeral I stood in the church where Zac grew up, listening to the priest talk about his life. It was as if time collapsed right in front of me. I saw all the years of knowing him, from the very first moment, before I'd even met him, when I had the dream of his face surrounded by white lights, to this moment, staring down the aisle at his coffin. I had such clarity all at once, seeing our entire relationship together, from start to finish. It was surreal, and yet it also felt like a gift. From the moment I heard Zac's voice tell me he was standing on the other side with our son, it was as if somebody had shined a light into a dark corner of myself that I hadn't acknowledged for thirty years. I never expected the healing that would come from Zac's passing. In that moment of clarity, he gave me his forgiveness, he gave me his love, and he gave me his blessing. I was free to move on. Letting the secret out felt like I was leaning into the pain of what happened instead of running from it, so healing could finally come to that place inside me. And where there was once pain, now there was only love. Had he made a different choice and chosen me, we both would have had much different, perhaps better, lives. But now it was possible to accept the choices we'd both made, and to see how much we had still meant to each other.

Many things continued to happen in the week after Zac's funeral. I kept hearing Zac in my day-to-day life. Then I had a crazy, frightening dream in which I did a portion of a line of coke, and was high. I awoke completely freaked out because I hated the feeling of impairment I had in the dream. I don't drink or do any substances, so the feeling was alarming, and I was scared because I wasn't sure what significance the dream held. I called my friend Jayne a few days later and asked if she could help me decipher the dream and access any messages that I might have missed in all the emotional weight of the last few weeks. I needed to know if there was anything else that would help me heal from this experience.

Jayne tuned into Zac, and he shared with us what he had learned from the other side: He had to be paralyzed or he would have continued down the bad path he was on, finally reaching things much darker than drugs and addiction. The accident forced him to abandon that path, and he was able to accrue "good karma" in his life while also burning away the "bad karma" from previous lifetimes. He also shared what I already suspected; that I was correct, and had he chosen me, he would not have been paralyzed. We would have had a full life together. Our son would have come back, conceived a second time and this time born, and we would have had another child as well. After this revelation, Jayne continued channeling Zac's communication, saying, "His soul underestimated the power of the addiction and that surprised him. He sent that dream to you to try to explain what happened from his perspective. After you gave him the ultimatum he tried to quit the coke, but one evening he did half a line, and that was all it took. He was hooked again. He was also trying to tell you that he was high when he had the accident and fell at work, and that no one knew that. This is why he never complained about his life after the fall. He knew it was his own fault. His guides arranged the paralysis because his soul's goal was to clear his karma and not to create more. He said it was a really powerful lesson and he is sorry he let you down."

Jayne explained Zac's message, "When we break a soul contract it throws us into a powerful depression and changes the course of our soul's path. But broken contracts can happen because each person has free will." She continued, "You were originally supposed to open his heart in the life you would have had together. He was supposed to love, protect, and provide for you, and your love for each other would have kept him on the straight and narrow." Sadly, even though that was our souls' original intent, he sacrificed that possibility for both of us by succumbing to the power of the drugs and choosing them over me. As Jayne's channeling of our story revealed each part of Zac's experience, I felt like I was watching the saddest movie I had ever seen. But it was my movie and I had lived it. I finally understood why I felt lost all those years after Zac.

A little while after receiving Jayne's help, my son came to me one night and said, "Mom, you made the right decision. I would have had a horrible lifetime because of Dad's choice. I would have been addicted to drugs by the time I was a teenager, and I would have created too much karma. I didn't want another tough lifetime after our last one together on the Trail of Tears. It's all right. You did it for me." I cried the rest of that night as I remembered.

sunlit                                              2017

*My ancestors told me: "Of course you would come back to live during the time when women have come to take back their power. This coming era will be a time when women's power will be known again. Women will heal what's been done."*

# men and karma

After Zac, I felt like a lost soul with no direction. Like I never really had anything that mattered. The summer before my senior year, I met Darren. We became friends, but I didn't start dating him until I came home after graduation. Darren was young as well, and he lived at home with his parents and young son Ben, who was four years old. I felt a love for that little boy that I could not describe. I think I was making up for the loss I had suffered. Whenever the three of us went anywhere and I held Ben in my arms as he slept, a great love and peace would surround me. I felt like the three of us were already a family, and I was surprised at the connection. We were together until Ben turned eight years old. I expected Darren and I to marry soon and move in together to start our lives. I started giving him a hard time, bored with the lifestyle we led together when Ben was not around, seeing the same people in the same places. In reality, I was getting impatient with the relationship not moving forward. I was anxious to be a family with him and little Ben. In spite of my feelings, we never had a fight or disagreed. However, I remember his mother said to me at the time, "Marie, do not marry my son." I still don't know why she said that, or why he finally made the choices he did. But shortly after that, Darren ended the relationship. He told me, "You can't stay in this little world that I'm in. You're meant for bigger things."

After that, I was so angry that I didn't care who I dated. I was distraught over Zac, distraught over the loss of little Ben, and I figured I would never be in love again. Not knowing about my broken "soul contract," I blamed myself for bad choices and I knew there was no going back. I didn't know how my past lives figured in my current life yet. All I had was this overwhelming anger.

At this time, Ellen and Luke had two little boys, who became a huge part of my life. They were part of my healing, and I didn't even know. The younger one, Elis, had to have a lot of surgeries because he was born with a deformity. When these started, I began spending a lot of time with the family because Ellen needed me to be there to help. Elis was just two when he had to have his first major surgery. Ellen wouldn't leave the hospital until I showed up to take over watching him. When I was not at the hospital I was with his older brother, Shane. Being with those boys healed a lot of my underlying pain. My dear friends shared every part of their boys' upbringing with me, and I am truly grateful because their love filled a huge hole in my soul. These two boys became the sons I never had in this life, and fill my heart to this day. After this, I had the hardest lesson to learn and the biggest karmic obstacle to face: my relationship with Ken.

I met Ken at a time when I didn't really care about romantic relationships anymore. I threw myself into my work and built up a very strong career as a graphic designer. I was angry at life and was being rebellious. I felt that I would never fall in love again, so I should just find someone who could take care of me, had some money, and liked the finer things. In my soul contract with Ken, I would be facing some deep wounds that needed to heal. It was as if my guides were putting me on "cleanup duty" for other lifetimes since my soul contract with Zac was broken. Ken and I were connected through many prior lifetimes, and it was time to overcome that karma to take my power back.

One night, out at a dance club with friends, a stranger approached me to dance. My first instinct was to refuse, and I told him I would not dance with him. "No" popped out of my mouth before I realized it. I should have walked out right then and there, but I didn't. The evening progressed, and drinking and dancing lessened my resolve, so that by the time the stranger approached me for a second time and asked, "Will you dance with me now?" I agreed.

Ken romanced me, taking me out for expensive dinners, to the beach on warm days, and out dancing. We dated like this for three years, and then he arranged to take me to an island for the weekend. He rented a small plane and we flew there. We arrived and went straight to dinner, where he proposed down on his knee, in the middle of the restaurant, in front of everyone. He had secretly ordered a custom ring made for me. Everything appeared perfect. I was so shocked and surprised. With all the attention focused on me I felt like I had to say yes. I chose to fall for the illusion. In hindsight, the only excuse I have for ignoring my first instinct to avoid him is that my heart was numb.

Looking back, there were numerous red flags that I disregarded. I avoided my misgivings about the relationship by focusing on other things. All my friends were getting married then, and I didn't want to be too old when I did. I really wanted to "design" a wedding, like a big design project or something I would do for work. I designed my invitations and had them printed by the printing company for which I worked. I worked with a seamstress who created the dresses my bridesmaids wore, and I found the most gorgeous wedding dress made of raw silk. I booked the best photographer I could find. I wanted the wedding to be a perfectly designed piece of art. And it was, on the surface.

I now realize that during that time, I wasn't just missing signs out of hurt or distraction, I was completely ignoring my intuition. I was intentionally ignoring it because I was so angry. I thought I was angry with God, but deep down, I was actually angry at myself, for the choices I had made, around Zac, and the child we conceived together. I even blamed myself for the failed relationship with Darren. My rebellious side jumped into marriage with Ken as a way to express that anger. I didn't believe, then, that there were any karmic ties involved in this decision, but there were. In order to learn that, I had to experience it. I had to make decisions, take action, and come out on the other side, long before I would ever discover the reasons why. No one ever gets out of the soul "work" that they have to do when they come to a new life. We do, however, have some influence over how hard we make that work for ourselves. I had two opportunities presented to me in the last moments before the wedding to back out of this relationship, and a third right after the honeymoon. I did not act on any of them, and I wish I had.

All parents have a very tough "job," wanting to protect their children from harm but also knowing that they need to live their own lives (and make their own mistakes). My parents were no exception. The day before the wedding, my mother said to me, "Are you sure you want to do this? It's okay if you don't. We will just have a big party and let everybody take home the gifts." This was my first escape route. My parents, even after putting up the money for a huge wedding, invited me to call it off, guilt-free. Instead, we could just have a big party in celebration of me not getting married. My parents were not fond of Ken, but even that didn't deter me. I said no. I wanted to have that wedding.

When the moment arrived for me to walk down the aisle, I started to cry as I stepped in beside my father. I knew I didn't love Ken, but here I was, getting married anyway. Even beyond that, I cried from a place of deep pain that I did not understand. By the time I got up to the front of the church where Ken was standing, I was sobbing uncontrollably. I think it was fear, on top of everything else, that caused such a reaction. All of these feelings combined were definitely my intuition telling me to stop. The priest looked at me with concern and said, "Dear, are you sure you want to do this?" There it was: my second escape route.

I hesitated for a moment, again the center of everyone's attention, with three hundred and fifty people staring up at me at the altar of this huge Italian Catholic church. I felt each of those eyes on me, and felt I had no choice but to continue. I caved and blurted out, "No, I want to go through with it."

Ken seemed oblivious to the entire scene, as far as I could tell, even though he stood right there. My tears were from fear, though I didn't realize it; I was letting out the pain of ignoring my intuition. Ken seemed to think that the tears were because I was so happy to be marrying him. I had become so numb that I didn't recognize the signs of my unhappiness, though they seem obvious in the retelling. This would be such a tough lesson for me to live through, and I could have avoided it if I'd let myself pay attention. We come to these types of crossroads in our lives many times, and we can pick the easy, more enlightened route or the really hard route that will get these lessons ingrained in our body. I took the really hard route this time.

We left for our honeymoon immediately after the wedding, and woke in the Caribbean. Ken insisted I wake at 8 AM. After putting on a wedding for three hundred and fifty people and traveling all night, I was exhausted. I thought that for a few days at least you were supposed to stay in bed and rest on a honeymoon, while enjoying each other's company as husband and wife. I did not want to get up, so Ken plucked me out of bed and deposited me in a chair with a mimosa, videotaping all the while. I was not happy even once on the two-week honeymoon.

Shortly after we got back, we went to my parents' house. Ken did not hide the changed tone he now seemed to use with me, though he had never spoken to me that way in front of my parents before the wedding. When my parents saw the honeymoon video, they were horrified to see Ken use physical force to pull me from bed that first day, even though he'd played the gesture off as romantic with the camera and the drink in my hand. My mother took me aside before we left and said, "Don't you want to come home now?"

I still missed the significance of my parents' reaction. My mother's words were the third time I was given permission to opt out of my situation, but I still resisted. My Catholic upbringing had a huge influence on me, and I thought that I had made an unbreakable vow before God and the Church. The decision to stay initiated thirteen months of personal hell.

During those months, Ken was often unemployed. I carried us financially. As the year progressed, I didn't know what to do. We lived in a third floor apartment in the middle of the city, and the sweet, old couple downstairs watched as I walked by them many mornings while Ken yelled at me from the upstairs window. I was so embarrassed. Going to work became an escape.

That was when I turned to God for help. I began to pray. I started to go to church at lunchtime. There was a wonderful priest there whose sermons seemed to teach me the things I most needed to learn in that moment. He would occasionally meet with me after mass when I asked for help. I started to depend on him and his sermons to get me through each day. Then one day, I went to church at lunchtime as usual, and he wasn't there. I was shocked and upset. As I left, I encountered a church volunteer putting things away after mass, so I inquired as to the priest's whereabouts. The man told me that the priest had died in the night, with the book that he wrote his sermons from lying on his chest, *The Road Less Traveled* by M. Scott Peck. That man was an angel for me, because I was able to go out and buy that book after I spoke with him. I read it and cried and cried and cried over the loss of the priest.

Something changed in me that day. I went home with a purpose and built a small Christian altar in my living room. I started kneeling at it to pray every morning, doing my rosary while Ken still slept. I prayed to Mary and Jesus to help me. I still didn't believe I could leave the marriage, but I didn't know how I could continue without help or some sort of change.

Shortly after that, Ellen asked me to babysit Elis and Shane at my place overnight. I was thrilled. The boys came over and I got them all comfy in their sleeping bags. We settled in to watch a movie. Ken started screaming, slamming doors, and banging things in the other room. Shane and Elis were terrified. We had these big doors in the apartment that could close off the living room, where the boys and I were, so I got some blankets and a pillow for myself and shut us in for the night. I stayed with the boys until morning, so they would feel safe. Sometime during that long night, something clicked inside me. This was the final straw. Seeing the children's reaction and putting their needs before my own allowed me to recognize and stand up to behavior I had come to tolerate for myself.

My prayers became even more desperate after that night. A few nights later, lying in bed, I felt distraught. With my body positioned as close to the edge of my side of the bed as possible, I prayed and prayed for help. Then all of a sudden, I "heard" the Virgin Mother, Mary! Her words reverberated through my entire soul, which is the only way I can describe it. She reassured me, "I hear you. I am here with you."

I was so startled and shocked that I got flippant and asked, "Oh, is Jesus here too?"

Just as I asked, my soul seemed to shake inside my body, and Jesus said, "Yes, I am."

My fear, my constant companion since the wedding, instantly vanished. I had not imagined that it was even possible to lose that fear. Thinking back to the feeling of hearing their words in that moment still brings a chill up my spine. It was my first real contact with Spirit since I was younger, and this time it was on a physical level. I felt them in my soul and I heard them speak to me, there is no denying that. They wanted to make sure I knew that they were there, and that I did not think I had imagined it.

I never mentioned anything to Ken about any of this. I don't believe he even knew that I got up and prayed every morning, or attended church every day. Shortly after the visit from Mary and Jesus, I came home from work one day and Ken and I fought over finances. I could tell that something major had shifted in me, because when Ken became enraged, I no longer cared. I had plans to leave for the beach that weekend to spend time with my parents, my girlfriend Maya, and my cousin Wyn. I told him I would deal with it when I got back. He relented.

I packed up, left, and spent the entire weekend talking things out with my parents and my friends. We went over every little detail of what I was experiencing in my relationship and what was happening in my head each time. I told them what happened with Jesus and Mary. I told them about the night Elis and Shane stayed over. They tried to help me figure out what to do. Maya and Wyn had to leave on Sunday to go home, but I stayed there with my mom until Monday. My mom and I continued our discussion at length.

On Monday morning, I woke with a new clarity of mind. I said to my mother, "I cannot go back to Ken."

"Hallelujah!" she said. Then she went out to her car and came back clutching a lawyer's card that she had carried around for thirteen months. The lawyer was a woman, and the best in the city. I walked over to the pay phone on the next street, called and hired her on the spot. My next phone call was to Ellen and Luke. I told them that I needed to get everything out of my apartment, and they immediately responded that I could store everything in their garage. Then I called all the rest of my close friends in the city to ask for whatever help they could give me to move. Even though it was Monday, some of them actually left work early and made the hour-long drive to help me get out that day. I was so grateful!

Just from changing my outlook on the situation, more miracles continued to happen. Since Ken thought I was still down at the beach, he wasn't trying to keep tabs on me and was at work. Usually he came home for lunch, but I think the angels made sure he didn't that day. My mother and I drove back up from the beach to my apartment, met up with all my friends, and removed the contents of the eight-room apartment in two and a half hours. Nothing had been packed, we were moving things from the third floor, and I had a lot of stuff. It should not have been humanly possible to pack and empty that apartment in two and a half hours, but with divine assistance, we did it. The elderly couple downstairs hugged me goodbye and, with relief in their eyes, said sweetly, "Good for you. We will miss you, but we are proud of you for making this choice." I left Ken with his things, a futon to sleep on, and a farewell note. And I was gone.

Not even a week later, we were at the courthouse with our lawyers for a pretrial hearing. After moving out, I had had a long talk with my lawyer. She advised that we complete the divorce proceedings at pretrial rather than let it go to trial, saying that we could use Ken's initial shock to quickly push the divorce through to completion. She prepared all the necessary paperwork in advance. Her lawyer's instincts were correct; Ken agreed to the divorce that day.

Once the divorce was complete at pretrial, and only then, did it seem to sink in with Ken that he had lost me. He used every excuse to see me, and called repeatedly. I found myself back in court almost immediately, winning an order of protection. After that, I petitioned the church and was granted an annulment of the marriage. If only I had listened to Spirit, the marriage would never have happened in the first place. But, it was over now. I moved back into my family home to heal.

Fifteen years later, I worked with Jayne Gabrielle to heal the remnants of trauma from my relationship with Ken. Just after we started, I had a horrible nightmare with emotions and imagery that made no sense. In the dream, I saw a dead woman wearing a white shift. She was blonde, dirty, and there were huge flies all over her. It was a terrifying, eerie image. I told Jayne about this dream, and she helped me to delve deeper into it. By doing this, we could see that it was my ancestors showing me a connection between my experience in my marriage with Ken and events in a past life. With Jayne's help, I was able to remember and describe some of this lifetime, but the regression got too emotionally intense for me to see the memories clearly. It was something my soul did not want to remember. My ancestors, however, insisted that it was necessary for me to remember this life and see the details. Jayne encouraged me to look into that scene again and tell her what happened.

The image in my nightmare was from a lifetime with Ken that ended with my undiscovered body rotting in the basement of a multistory tenement building. Once I started to remember more details, the floodgates opened and other, earlier contracts with Ken's soul were revealed to me. According to my memories, he had been abusive with me over many lifetimes, murdering me many times. In one Native life, he had thrown me off a cliff. In another lifetime shortly after that, I lived in London and became a craftswoman who created beaded lamps and dresses popular during the Art Nouveau era. I was not Native, but had inherited knowledge and skill in beadwork retained from previous Native lifetimes. I made a good living at it; even then, I was a woman with a career. Ken and I had two little towheaded children in that lifetime: a boy and a girl. In a rage one night, Ken killed me and threw my body into the corner of the basement. The murder went undetected until the smell of my decomposing flesh started to fill the building. Upon the discovery of my corpse, my killer pretended to help the men remove my body from the tenement basement, as if he were the distraught husband who didn't know what had happened to his wife! My spirit was so angry seeing this because Ken made sure that my body was not covered when it was brought out of the basement, so that my children witnessed it. He wanted my rotting body to be the last image of me in their minds. Infuriated, I would not cross over, and instead became an angry ghost. My ancestors told me that I tormented him to the extreme. Finally, I scared Ken so badly one night that I drove him into the street and into the path of an oncoming carriage, killing him. I tormented him to death because he continued to abuse our children. I was trying to save them. My mother was also present in that lifetime. She lived across the city but worked nearby as a cleaning lady at a neighborhood church. My children were given to her after Ken's death. When they were safe, I moved on.

As Jayne and I put the pieces together to understand my past stories, my current one started to make sense. Because Ken's previous incarnations had taken my life with impunity so many times before, I needed to break free from him this time around, to finally save my life and reclaim my power as a woman. It was residual fear of him from those past lives that had clouded my judgment and allowed me to enter into the marriage despite my feelings of doubt. But it was also Elis and Shane who triggered me to find the courage to break the cycle, because my experience with them paralleled my experience with my own children in those past lives. When I was able find the strength to break the cycle for myself, the universe seemed to line up to help me resolve the karmic ties. I am still so grateful and relieved that this chapter of my soul's learning is closed. I took my power back!

maine                                                                1998

*In a vision, one of my Native grandmothers said to me, "Don't be embarrassed by your humanness. You are doing just fine. To know God, you must seek him in all the things in life that you love."*

## moving forward

After I recovered from the divorce, artwork started to flow through me again. I started to paint, and then I created jewelry out of recycled leather I had accumulated. I expanded to decorating mirrors and covering old cigar boxes. I would carve designs into them and add accents of beads. This is when I started my side business named "Peau Charmant." My mother and I came up with that name one morning. "Peau Charmant" means "pleasant leather" in French. I showed and sold my work at a few fairs and art shows in the area, and that was just the beginning. I also felt a new sense of freedom at being released from my situation at home. I went whitewater rafting, skydiving, and started racing on a ski team. I became an adrenaline junky, daring God to catch me in my life, both figuratively and literally. I felt exhilarated and safe, and I was enjoying every moment.

My primary job was at a printing company in Massachusetts, and I loved it. I worked with amazing designers, and this was a special time in my life. My job was like a second home to me. I loved all my coworkers; they felt like family, and I loved to go to work. We were a talented design team and became longtime friends. We worked hard together and had become a well-oiled, successful machine. Then — bam! — the company was sold to new ownership. We were all distraught. Many of my coworkers lost their jobs, and the rest of us were merged with another company and moved. I did not like the changes we were forced to make, especially the change in location to a city that now saddled us with a merciless commute. We all felt betrayed.

After a year of enduring this new corporate environment, I started to look for a new job but I wasn't receiving any offers. I got so disgusted that one day, after an incredibly bad commute into work, I walked into my dark cubicle and with intense emotion I said to God, "That's it! I want to be where there is ocean and woods!" I meant it so vehemently that I accidentally manifested it. I did not know then that any prayer said with such conviction and emotion causes its immediate manifestation. Just moments after speaking aloud to God, I opened up a periodical that listed jobs in my industry and discovered a small ad for the position of art director in Maine. I packed up some samples with my resume and shipped them off in response. I got a call right away from the owner of the company. She arranged for me to travel to meet with her at the design firm and to stay for the weekend to visit the area.

The next morning while on my way to my interview, I drove through the little town where the company was located and I distinctly heard, "You're going to live here. You have the job." I felt so certain that this was where I was supposed to go, that I didn't question or doubt anything. From there, everything else fell into place. The owner found me a cute little apartment right in town, and I moved there without a thought. It felt right. My parents helped me on the day that I moved in, but after they left at the end of the day I was completely alone for the first time to start my new life. I started working at the new job and I loved it. I made new friends instantly, and it felt to me as though this little town in Maine had truly welcomed me. One evening I was talking to my sister on the phone when she asked me, "How can you do that? How can you just pick up and move away to somewhere you've never been and then make friends like you have?" I didn't know how to answer her then, and I was shocked at what I had created with that one prayer. Now, with understanding, I know that I was guided by the assurance that I was on the right path.

After a few weeks, I settled into a routine and then more fortuitous things started to happen. There was a little bookstore in town, and when I would go in to shop I started having my attention called to certain books that I needed to read. My ancestors began waking me up in the middle of the night by talking to me, which scared me half to death. I started having dreams about bears. In these dreams the bears were chasing me and I would become more and more afraid until I woke up. I tried to process these dreams and messages, but being new in town, there was no one close by whom I trusted to talk to about it. One morning I finally felt so over-whelmed by the dreams and the messages that I walked right into my new boss's office, sat down, and told her that I needed to talk.

I don't know what possessed me to open up to her, but I told her everything that was happening. I told her about the books I had never seen or been interested in before that were now suddenly catching my attention. I told her about the voices waking me in the night, and that I was scared, being in a new and strange place alone. She had a curious expression on her face at first but then she smiled at me. I didn't know what made me decide to share this or think that I could trust her, but she was spiritually connected and was not shocked by my words. She calmed me down and started to explain a little bit of what was happening to me. She was involved with a group of women who practiced Native American spiritual ways, and she recognized that the dreams and messages I was receiving were aligned with that spirituality. I then revealed to her that I was part Native American.

Amina and I laugh about this now, when we reminisce. Here she was, my new boss and a business owner, and I came into her office completely freaked out by supernatural experiences and sat down and laid them all out on the table as if I knew her and knew she would understand. Of course, later I would learn this was because my soul did know her, but at the time I could have easily expected a very different reaction.

My spirit grandfather has since told me that this was the point in my life where they could fully reach out to me because I was the most open to them. It was the first time that I was away from my Italian family, and there was room for me to hear them without distractions. Even though I felt comforted by Amina, I was still very uneasy at night by myself. Shortly after I told Amina, I told my cousin Wyn what was going on and that I was afraid, and she came up to stay with me for the weekend. We decided to attend a local Catholic church service on Sunday morning while she was there, and during the mass the priest was doing things a little differently than I was used to. He was incorporating some Native American messages. I was astonished that any Catholic priest would do this. I was so impressed by him that I went up to thank him after the mass was finished. When I walked up to him at the back of the church and met his eyes, I felt as if I already knew him. The feeling was so strong it was overwhelming, and he felt it as well. I told him that I needed to come and talk with him. He looked me in my eyes and said, "Yes you do." I was so overwhelmed by emotion that I left my purse in the church and had to go back to retrieve it.

Shortly after that, I made an appointment to go meet with him. As we talked, I learned that he had just moved to the area from a reservation where he had been assigned as a priest for ten years. His experience there had opened his mind to Native interpretations of spirituality. He patiently explained to me how God and my ancestors were working through the dreams I was having and the messages I was hearing. He comforted me, assuring me that the devil wasn't after me or tricking me. These experiences were just my ancestors trying to reach me. As we spoke about this, the veil between worlds must have thinned in response to our conversation, because Jesus and my Native grandfather appeared before both of us. Jesus took my hand and walked me over to Grandfather, put my hand into Grandfather's and said, "They will teach you now. Do not be afraid." Then the vision was over and Jesus and Grandfather vanished.

The priest and I sat there, shocked and without words, as if time stood still. Jesus was giving me his blessing to move forward on this Native spiritual path, and he did it with the priest as witness so that I would know it was real and not just in my own mind. This vision gave me the courage I needed to start down the path to discover who I was and who my ancestors were.

After this vision, I started reading the books I had been drawn to, like *Bury My Heart at Wounded Knee* by Dee Brown, and other histories of Native people written by Native writers. I was learning the truth of what had happened to us from our own people, and I hadn't known any of this history before. I was so upset to find that what I had been taught in school was largely inaccurate, and had been told from a perspective that glossed over the more horrendous acts of the settling Europeans in favor of painting a patriotic vision of American greatness. This was when I began researching my family's personal history as well, finding paperwork from my aunt and an older cousin who had also heard the family story from her parents and had done research into our genealogy. My grandparents had passed away by this time, and I had no one left to ask who remembered the older generations. As I dug, I didn't realize how deep our family wounds ran. Yet, as I began uncovering information, it was as if my ancestors were handing me the books to read one by one as I could handle them.

My intuitive abilities got stronger during this time as well, because the meeting with the priest and the vision had helped to eliminate my fear. Without this fear I was engaging and listening more actively, and began learning more about the gifts I had. During all this time of transition, I had been dating a man, Jay, who worked at the printing company I had left. It was really more of a friendship, but Jay would come up to visit me once a month or so. I started having dreams of him dying, and though I was no longer afraid of the dreams, I became very concerned about what they meant for him. Then one night I was woken up from a sound sleep by a loud, commanding male voice yelling, "Break up with him! Break up with him now!" I felt like I jumped three feet off the bed in fright. After realizing it was my Native grandfather, my breathing steadied and I could focus on what he was saying to me. For the first time I was able to distinctly hear the command and recognize it for what it was, so I listened. I was also beginning to understand that my gut feeling was another of their means of reaching out to me, and I now believed that if they were telling me something like this, it must be for a reason.

I had already been planning to visit Jay that weekend, so I wrote a letter explaining why we needed to break up that I would hand him in person. We didn't fight, and it was a pretty comfortable relationship, so I felt I needed to delicately explain to him why we couldn't stay together. We had decided to meet at a Mexican restaurant in his town, and when I walked in he was at the bar waiting for me. He had started a conversation with the guy next to him. When I reached them both, the guy looked up at me and said, "He just told me that you were going to walk in and break up with him. Is that true?" I was so shocked that I didn't answer him. I just grabbed Jay's arm and led him to our table.

After we settled in, I handed Jay the letter as we ate. He read it and we talked into the night. Jay did not believe that I had gifts and would not acknowledge or even entertain that fact. During our discussion that evening, he seemed elusive and would not answer any of my questions directly. Finally, at about two in the morning, he broke down and started being honest. Jay said to me, "How did you know?"

"How did I know what?" I replied.

"How did you know I was doing crack?" He asked. I said, "I didn't. I just have had dreams of you dying, and my Grandfather told me to break up with you." Although I had discussed these abilities with him on prior occasions, in this encounter I realized Jay didn't believe me and wasn't satisfied with this explanation. Even though that might not have been the closure Jay wanted, I think breaking up with him actually saved his life in the end. He went into rehab and was able to get clean.

Shortly after I ended the relationship with Jay, a Native American woman came to my small Maine town and was teaching about spiritual ways. I spent some time learning from her while she was there. At one meeting, she saw my Native ancestors standing around me and encouraged me to research their names and who they had been in life, in order to find out more about who I was. She also told me that my ancestors were calling me to do a vision quest, and she explained what that was. I would need to go to a mountain, or somewhere remote in the woods, for four days and four nights with just a sleeping bag and a drum and rattle. I was to stay there until I received a vision for my life. They were calling me to do this, so again I listened. She told me that she would oversee my vision quest, but when the time came, she had made plans to travel and would not be there. She told me that she would still guide me from wherever she was going to be. I later learned that the medicine person who is overseeing your vision quest is supposed to remain close to the area that you're in for the whole four days, to keep an eye on you for your safety. My ancestors were not happy with her for not being there.

One weekend in October, I made my way deep into the woods of Maine, alone. I had never done anything like this before. I had never been in the woods alone, without a camper or my family or friends. I wasn't very afraid, however, because I had an overwhelming feeling of newfound trust in my ancestors. I had made sure that a couple of my friends knew where I was going to be for those four days, so I felt that they would know where to come look for me if I didn't return as planned.

I was apprehensive but excited at what might occur during those next four days. After everything that I had witnessed in the last few months, I had high expectations for a supernatural experience. I gathered as many rocks as I could carry along the trail. I was looking for the right spot that would suit me for the four days. Just as I came to an enclosed area under a large pine tree at the top of the hill, a hawk flew directly over me. I took it as a sign and offered tobacco. Using the stones I had carried and others I found close by, I created a Stone Circle for protection around this selected spot. For the center of the circle, I found a very large, flat rock that seemed perfect for the fire. I would have to keep a fire going continuously for the four days. The area also seemed safe to me because the surrounding brush meant that nothing could sneak up behind me in the dark without being heard, and during the day I could see all the way around me. I was told to pay close attention to any animals that appeared to me and to try not to be afraid of them, because they would be bringing me messages and I would be protected by Spirit.

Once all my preliminary tasks were completed, it wasn't too long before I started getting restless in my circle. I was high energy and not very grounded at the time, so to sit there and pray for hours was quite a task for me. I got bored quickly and I kept waiting for something to happen. I tried to let the peace of the woods envelop me, but I was too antsy. I began contemplating why I was there, who I really was, and why I was called to do this.

During the first night, I was terrified. I kept the fire going all night and sang the few Native songs I had learned, drumming and rattling until morning. My hearing became incredibly sharp, and tuned instantly to the slightest noise. In the morning, I watched as a red fox chased a squirrel right past me. They didn't even see me as they went right by me in my circle.

After the brief excitement of the fox, I felt as though time slowed down. The minutes seemed like hours as day turned into night. The next day moved just as slowly, but I continued to pray. Then, late into the third night, a barred owl swooped down and screeched just above my head. It sounded like a woman screaming. I think I must have jumped five feet off the ground. My heart felt as if it were pounding out of my chest, and I continued to feel uneasy the rest of the night. I could sense that there was a "mystical" energy around me, and I was on edge. I heard many more animals rustling all around me, after the owl, but I could see none of them. Hours later, I heard something much larger making its way toward me. I jumped up and immediately started to stoke the fire, cutting my hand fairly deeply in the process.

The next morning I heard a woman's voice say, "Well, we told her to come and she's here. What are we going to do now?!" I later understood that my ancestors were frustrated with the woman who was supposed to be overseeing my vision quest, and I overheard this part of the conversation. On various occasions after hearing the woman's voice, I also saw what looked like ripples of water in the air, all around the perimeter of the circle. The sky at sunset was bright orange, almost the same color as the fire in front of me, and I felt, again, the same "mystical" energy surrounding me. In that moment, it felt like my ancestors' protection.

On the fourth day I was getting weak and tired, but my fear was completely gone. After hearing my ancestors' voices and feeling their protection, I no longer felt the constant fear I had on the previous three days. I had brought a jug of water with me but it was gone on the first day. I didn't know how to plan for my needs well enough, so by the fourth day I had been without water for three days. I felt drawn to leave my circle, and I moved to the nearby cliff. I smudged and prayed, and I remember hearing the name "Red Bear." I wasn't sure who that name belonged to. Not yet having learned his name, I thought it might be my spirit grandfather's. I was so tired and weak by then, but I still managed to make my way back down to civilization. I was greeted by Amina and my friend Kay, and I was so grateful to see them. They gave me broth and took good care of me after my four day adventure. I was so disappointed and thought that nothing substantial had really happened, but in reality much did. I received many messages, but they were subtle and I was not used to subtle. Only in hindsight did I realize how profound those four days would be for me in my life. Spirit was speaking to me through signs I hadn't yet learned to recognize. Even the fact that I could hear my ancestors audibly was a big deal, and a new "normal" I was only starting to get used to.

A week or so later, my ancestors told me that I had not really completed my vision quest because I had left the stone circle and gone up on the cliff on the fourth day. They told me I had to go back up the hill and spend one more day in the stone circle to complete the vision quest. It was cold on the day I returned. I had buried the stones when I left it, not knowing I would need them again. As I approached, I felt a tingling go through my entire body. I walked into the circle and there, right where I had sat for all those days, was a bear's paw print, larger than both my hands together, clear and deep in the mud and ice. I was in awe as I sat down in front of this single, perfect print, with no other signs of disturbance around it. Channeling this emotion, I drummed and prayed for a few hours.

All of a sudden I heard Grandfather tell me in a stern voice, "You need to leave now!"

I said out loud in response, "But you told me I had to stay all day to complete my quest!"

He responded, "You leave now!" So I packed up and left. As I trekked down the hill, it started to snow, getting heavier and heavier as I hiked down. By the time I reached the bottom, I was in a whiteout. There was a blizzard that day in Maine that came with no warning. I was learning to trust my spirit grandfather, and learning to understand that he was protecting me and I should heed his guidance without question.

As this experience was helping me to become more at home with my gifts and my guides, I was also becoming more at home in this Maine town. I started exploring my art even more during the quiet winters, and in the evenings after work. I began creating these stone and metal pieces that I called "Grounding Spirals," in the form of stone sculptures and necklaces. My ancestors told me that their hands are over my hands when I make these and that each one is a healing piece being made for one person in particular. I would be the keeper of each piece until the person it was meant for happened to purchase it, or it was bought for them as a gift. Only then would each piece leave me. I have now been making these for over twenty years. My stone sculptures have evolved over time to include crystals and minerals, but each piece is still made in deep meditation and for one particular person. I have made over 500 of these over the years and each one has always found its home.

I also continued to delve deeper into Native spirituality after the vision quest. I had many chance meetings with people, friends, and extended family who became significant throughout the rest of my life. I went to pow wows, and I was diligent in attending any ceremony I was invited to. In this way, I was being guided deeper into my past and identity than ever before, and was being taught more and more by both my ancestors and the amazing teachers they arranged for me to meet along the way. From this town in Maine, I traveled all over the eastern part of Canada, literally being guided by my grandfather and ancestors to locations I couldn't find again if I tried. I went to a town called Matane on the Gaspé Peninsula, where I found information indicating that was where my family was from. Grandfather told me that the connection I seek is somewhere in that town, sitting in a family bible in someone's attic, and someday in the future, when that family starts to trace their roots, I will be able to make the connection with them. I am still waiting on that one.

After living and working in the small Maine town for five years, I went into work one day and was told the company was relocating. I was so upset and had an uneasy feeling about the entire move. I did not want to leave that town. Eventually, I had to get used to the idea. With the company leaving, there were no other opportunities in my field there, so there was no way I could stay. I started making preparations for the move and went down to the city to start looking for an apartment. I signed a rental agreement and decided to go see the new office.

As I walked in the door of the new office building my grandfather said to me, "You will never work here!"

I was shocked, and answered him with "Really?! I just put down the deposit on the new apartment!" I wasn't trying to be disrespectful to the message, but I was thinking "you couldn't have told me a little sooner before I put the deposit down?!"

The office space was empty, since nobody was working there full time yet. I walked over to a table and happened to find the latest periodical that had current job listings. There was one ad for an assistant creative director position back home. I was really angry that I was being forced to move from a place I loved. I decided that if I was going to be moved, it was going to be on my terms. That being the case, I half-heartedly applied for the position. I grabbed some samples of my work and a résumé, put a sticky note on top that said "if I look like a good asset to your company, give me a call" and I mailed it in response to the ad.

I really didn't expect an answer since I hadn't put my heart into the application, but I was still really angry about leaving. After five years I had really settled into that job, and that little town had become so special to me. I had people there that I had adopted as a second family, and many other new friends besides. On top of all of that, the message I received walking into the new office had thrown me for a loop. But then, the same week that I mailed that application, I came home for lunch one day and the phone rang. It was the president of the company I had applied to, and he wanted me to come down to meet with them. I told him I was going on vacation to Rhode Island the last week of August, which was only a couple of weeks away, and we made an appointment for me to come in and interview on my way through. When I went to the meeting, I discovered that their creative director had contacted me when I worked at my prior job. It was strangely coincidental and we both remembered that connection.

During the interview I was impressed with the caliber of design work they were doing, but as I was showing them my work, I realized how much I still loved the company that I worked for. I decided that I wouldn't take the new job if it was offered, and felt that I was at least slightly more in control by making that decision. I went on my vacation, but I could not relax because everything was still changing for me. I was completely uncomfortable being pulled from somewhere I loved and forced into the unknown, and now I knew I was going to have to make yet another choice if they offered me this position. And they did.

This was the era before cell phones, so we had a pay phone down at the beach that we used when we needed to make a call or touch base with home. When I called to check my messages, I had one from the company asking me to call them back, so I did. They requested a second interview, and I interrupted the vacation to travel back for it. This time, I was even more convinced that I wouldn't take the job. When their general manager started to discuss salary with me, I had a bit of an attitude. I wasn't trying to be egotistical, but I really didn't want to move back, so I was subconsciously trying to slightly sabotage the interview. He tried playing the money game with me, offering a lower starting salary, but I wouldn't have it. I told him I was not going to move twice, so they needed to make a decision quickly because I was either moving there or to the city with my current company. When he asked me what I wanted for money I requested what was basically double my current salary, thinking they would never go for it. I left and enjoyed the last two days of my vacation, stopping at my sister's on the way home. When I got to my sister's, I called in to check my messages, and I had three from the president of the company; two with his office number and one with his home number. All three urgently requested that I call him right back. I called him back and he offered me the job for almost the exact amount I had asked for, and being unable to say no to such an increase in salary, I took the job.

Though I had initially felt I was being forced into change, I now felt like this was a new beginning for me and was eager to see what would happen. Though I was still impatient about many things at that age, I had not dated anyone in years. With my dating history, I was convinced that I had made huge, irreversible mistakes in my life with all that had transpired. I figured that the choices I made had messed up my personal life beyond repair, but at least my professional life was working out well. I regretted the choices I had made with men, and thought that I had missed my opportunity for "true love" and was destined to be alone without a family. Although I had started to understand my heritage and its spiritual ways, I still lacked the understanding of why I had to live through what I did. When I moved back to Massachusetts, I got a small apartment in the basement of a couple's home, and settled in to start my new job. The rent was cheap, and my plan was to save money to buy a house.

Manny owned the house across the street from where I was renting. The couple who lived upstairs from me were friends with him, and they often had a communal campfire in the evenings to hang out together. They invited me to join them one night, and that's how I met him. We became friends over the course of a few months, and then one day he asked if I wanted to go with him for a ride on his motorcycle and out to dinner. We found that we had some things in common that we liked to do. I grew up fishing and hunting with my dad, and Manny was an outdoorsman. We began dating and would go out fishing on his boat or on motorcycle rides. I wasn't "in love" with him but I enjoyed his company and we were having fun together.

As planned, during this time I had been working and saving money to buy my first house. About a year later I had a dream. In this dream, I had a glimpse of a sign on a building with the name of a local town, and when I awoke I became convinced that my guides were telling me the name of the town where I would find my house, and to start looking for a home of my own. Since my job was secure and I had saved enough, I started house hunting. My mom joined me on this new adventure and I began looking in the town I believed I had been guided to. I found a local real estate agent, and my mom and I were enjoying touring different homes. Though we were having fun, I still couldn't find a house that I wanted.

Then one afternoon, we traveled down a new road for the first time and I saw the sign. My agent had set up a showing for a house and we were supposed to meet her there, having only the address for reference. On our way to the appointment we came upon a different house for sale, and for a moment I thought it was the one we were scheduled to see. This one was just down the road and, having just gone on the market, had only had a sign put up that day. It was the perfect house for me, and I shortly discovered it was also just down the road from the sign I had seen in my dream. In actuality, the town name was part of the name of the business that had put up the sign, but the building itself was not actually located in the town. My mom and I had a laugh over that but figured the sign was just meant to be confirmation that it was the right choice. I decided to go ahead and buy the house.

Now I realized that I had to tell Manny I had bought a house and was moving. I had been thinking the relationship wasn't serious and we were just having fun, because he had stated before that he would never get married. I wasn't in love with him, so I believed him and didn't think he was in love with me either. It was fine with me that we were just friends. However, shortly after I broke the news that I would be moving, I was in for a surprise.

He started acting differently within a few weeks. I didn't understand the change in character. Then one day he got down on his knee and proposed to me. I was shocked. At first, I didn't know what to say. At this time I still believed that love was no longer out there for me, so I thought, "Well, maybe companionship is the next best thing." So I said yes. I'm sure my spirit grandfather was shaking his head as I headed for yet another life lesson. Grandfather later told me that Manny had changed his mind about marriage when his perception of me became like that of the "winning horse in a race." Manny figured if he was ever going to take a chance at marriage, it was me.

Once we were married, everything was "okay." Especially in comparison to my previous marriage. However, Manny soon started to get bigger and bigger "toys" because of the income I was bringing in. I started to feel more like his parent than a partner. One beautiful afternoon Manny and I took my parents out for a fishing trip on our boat. It was a beautiful day, and in that moment I had everything I wanted, but something still felt so off. While my dad and Manny were distracted by fishing at the stern of the boat, my mom and I were watching the water at the bow. All of a sudden I said to her, "Shouldn't I be happy? I have everything I could want. Why do I feel so unhappy inside?" My mother just looked at me and said, "Yes, you should be, but you'll have to look inside to see why you're not." I contemplated this for a while after that conversation. I poured myself into my work again as I tried to identify exactly what was wrong. Although things weren't bad between us, I began to realize I had made yet another mistake because I wasn't interested enough in Manny as a partner.

Though I was starting to have doubts about this marriage, I still enjoyed my job at the same well-known design firm that got me to move home, only now as assistant creative director. I loved being a designer and that was where I felt confident. One day my dear friend, who was the creative director, gave his notice. I was upset that he was leaving, but I took the opportunity to walk into the president's office and ask him directly if I would move into the position of creative director for the firm. He told me absolutely yes. I believed him until a couple of weeks later when a new creative director showed up to work. He was a young guy from an ad agency in Boston, someone who could "talk the talk with the boys" and with the salesmen. Oh, and he was a *man*! He was secretly hired for the position I was told was mine. I met him on the day he started, and I immediately drafted up my resignation and walked back into the president's office and handed it to him. He looked up at me in disbelief and shock, and I said to him, "You lied to me. I'm going out into business on my own." He didn't know what to say. They had been marketing the company based on my design work, and had never expected I would leave such a salary quickly enough that they wouldn't have a chance to persuade me to stay.

When I made that leap to start my own business, I was scared. I was leaving a solid, high-paying position, and even though I didn't have a non-compete clause with the firm, I decided, out of integrity, to not go after any of their clients when I walked away. I walked out on faith and I was tested. When my prior firm heard I was out on my own, they asked that I start freelancing for them again, and I was able to get by pretty well.

Two years later I got a call from a contact at one of the large corporations in Connecticut. The founder was disgusted with the work from my old firm after I left, so the following year they hired a big agency in New York city, which they ended up not being happy with either. Next, the founder had stormed into the board meeting asking, "Where is that girl that did our annual reports?! Find her!" And that's when my contact called me. This was a pivotal point in my business. From then on I did all their annual reports and marketing, and from that starting point I built my business up.

After I left, my former design firm had continued to use my design work to sell the company's capabilities, even though I was no longer there. They did this for a couple of years. I never heard from them in all that time, until one of the clients insisted that they hire me as a designer and they were forced to call me. By then my own business was well established. I told their salesman that I had to think about it and I would call him back with my decision the next day.

I had a lot of anger when I left that company. I felt betrayed, and I had said to myself that it would be a cold day in hell the next time I worked for them. But I decided to pray about it, and I talked about it with my friend, the creative director who had left. The next morning a funny thing happened. When I went out to take my dog for a walk in the early morning hours, it was snowing. Everything was covered in white, and when I looked into my backyard it looked like the woods behind it were on fire. There was a building on fire on the next road, but I mistakenly thought my woods were on fire because it was so bright. When I realized what was actually happening and took in the entire scene, I started to laugh in spite of it, because it dawned on me that it looked like hell had frozen over in my own backyard. Everything had aligned for me to be standing there in that moment, witnessing these occurrences come together to present an image from my own words to me as a sign. So I said, "I get it. I forgive them." I called the firm back that morning and did the one project for them. When it was complete, I went to the company and walked in proudly to deliver it and pick up my check. I ran smack into my old boss who had lied to me, and he could barely look me in the eye. In that moment, I felt as though some karmic payback had happened, and I was able to let this all go and move on.

Following this, Manny and I parted ways at the five year mark of our marriage. Despite my focus on work, I still knew on some level that I was not happy with him. As a means of moving on, I continued to expand my business, and also opened up an art gallery in Rhode Island and ran my design firm from there. After our marriage came to a conclusion, my ancestors shared with me the karmic tie I had with Manny, which helped to clarify my feelings toward him in our present relationship. After the end of the marriage, I had been working with Jayne again to figure out what I was doing wrong in my relationships. What was it in me that still needed to be healed? My ancestors came through during a session with Jayne where I was struggling for answers. They told me that in a past lifetime our roles were reversed. I was the husband and he was the wife. We couldn't have children because something was physically wrong. I was away frequently to hunt for food, and over time I met another woman along the way. Since I was unable to have children in my marriage and I was unsure about who had the physical problem, I took liberties and ended up with children from this new union. "Manny" had never known of the other relationship or children until the day of my funeral when they were all there at the service. She had looked out over the crowd after the service was over and saw a family she did not recognize. As she saw each of the children's faces with my resemblance, the realization finally dawned on her. I was on the other side, watching this with an initial feeling of relief that I had not been caught. That was short-lived. I then had to face my life review, and had to feel how others felt as I stood in their shoes and felt each of their emotions. I had to live through the betrayal and pain that I caused Manny in that life. In this life, I had to heal that karmic tie with Manny in order for us to move on. Although, Grandfather liked to joke, "You didn't have to go so far as to marry him!"

After my broken soul contract with Zac, I felt like a lot of these relationships, as well as the career moves, were a rearranging of my life. Like I was a puzzle piece being moved around to accommodate my mission or soul purpose. Had Zac made the other choice, Grandfather told me he would have followed along this Native healing path with me, which is called the "Red Road." But following this path was inevitable in my case, even without him, and since he was not there with me, it left space for these other karmic ties with Jay and Manny to be healed. The Red Road is who I am and it is how I serve myself and others. Even though things had felt chaotic to me much of the time, I was working on a coherent project to clean up karma and make the most of this particular lifetime after my soul contract did not go as planned. A soul's purpose remains the same, even if we disrupt the initial game plan by making bad choices with our free will. This can give us hope, knowing that even if we make mistakes, we will be helped back onto the right path.

vision quest                    1997

*I had a dream and I woke up with a word that I had never heard before: "Kachagawa (Ka-Sha-gaw-wa)." I do not know for certain how to spell it. I do not know what tribal language it is from. I only know how it sounds when I say it. I was told when I woke up from that dream that I was "wolf clan" then. It was from a memory of another lifetime that I had tapped into, but that is all the information I was told. This word is still a mystery to me. There is some connection to the tribal language that it comes from, but I still do not know what that is.*

# remembering

The first of my past lives that I was allowed to remember were not pleasant ones. After living in Maine for a while, I discovered that the area I lived in had distinct ley lines. Ley lines, according to Wikipedia, *"are apparent alignments of land forms, places of ancient religious significance or culture, often including man-made structures. They are ancient, straight 'paths' or routes in the landscape which are believed to have spiritual significance."* This is likely why I had such a transformation while I lived there. Healers of many different modalities, some that I had never even heard of, were drawn to that area. I encountered massage therapists, craniosacral therapists, shamanistic healers, and the like. I had been struggling with my own gifts before I was drawn to Maine, and I was still struggling to get my focus and understand how these gifts made me a bridge between worlds after I moved there. Since I was surrounded by so many spiritual people, I went to visit with a shamanistic healer right after I moved there. I was very skeptical and I didn't know what I was walking into. She was not Native, and I had always thought that shamans were supposed to be Native. However, I had heard of her skills through word-of-mouth, so I thought I would try seeing her.

Since I was not yet in touch with my own gifts, I was way out of my comfort zone with this woman. To my surprise, this visit turned out to be unlike anything I had ever experienced, and I know that I surprised her as well. She guided me into a deep meditation and asked me to describe where I was. I told her I was in a primitive cabin, deep in the woods. As I looked closer, I realized that I was chained like an animal. The chains only allowed me to go a short distance, into the area surrounding the cabin. The need to escape overwhelmed me, and this feeling developed into intense panic. I felt the complete and full force of this panic, maybe because it re-awakened memories that had scared me as a child in this life.

When I first started describing the scene, it took me a few moments to get my bearings and comprehend it. I quickly went from seeing through the eyes of this woman and experiencing the weight and feel of the chains, to being pulled out of my body and seeing the memory shift so I was able to view and describe it as if watching a movie. I could see from above that there was a trapper traveling towards the Native woman on the chain. As I witnessed the scene, I remembered him and knew him to be a Frenchman. It seemed as though he had been gone for days. The woman had a look of fear and desperation on her face as he approached. He put his things down, dragged her by the hair into the cabin, and raped her.

As the vision progressed, things seemed to happen faster and faster. I saw many scenes where the Trapper packed and left. He would leave her for days at a time. During his absence, other trappers would come and rape her. The cabin seemed to be located in the north of Canada, because everybody spoke French. There was a record player or gramophone in the cabin that played classical music. That music was played often while she was being raped. One day, a small Frenchman arrived while the Trapper was away. He seemed to have compassion for her and helped her escape. The next scene I remembered was her with this man in a small town. There was a newly built railroad station. I remember getting into a railroad car. Once on board, I was overcome with a huge sense of relief. That is when the shamanistic healer guided me out of the meditation.

I was quite freaked out by this experience. I didn't understand what I saw. At first, I thought it was not my memory and that the shaman had not helped me at all. When I started working with Jayne many years later, I learned that it was my Native spirit grandfather who had channeled to me what I had seen, and that I had many recent lifetimes which were extremely hard and similar to that one. I had lived through much, and as I grew to be able to handle the memories, they would reveal them to me. This memory was particularly grueling and had occurred during the "occupation." The occupation is what Grandfather called it when the Europeans came to take over our land.

That particular lifetime was a connection to my most recent boyfriend at the time, Jay. Jay had been the Frenchman that saved me. That was part of the reason that Grandfather had woken me up in the middle of the night and told me to break up with him. In a way, I had to save him from himself in this life. It was a karmic tie and an agreement we had made before being born. When Grandfather started revealing these things to me, I started to understand how thin the veil is between lifetimes, and how intricately previous lifetimes interconnect to things in my current life. Even before this memory was revealed, I could never listen to classical music. Anytime it played anywhere around me, I would cringe and be inexplicably uncomfortable. Whenever my mother put on classical music in the house when I was young, I would scream and cry and make her shut it off. Just last week, when I was talking to her on the phone, she had classical music playing on the radio in the background. I couldn't continue the conversation. I asked her to shut it off and said that it was extremely distracting to me and not in a good way. She said, "You still haven't grown out of that? I would think by now you would have an appreciation for classical music." I can't really explain to her that this aversion is like a cellular memory in my body that I can't erase. Even though my mom knows all about my gifts, it's hard for her and other people to comprehend how I live between worlds, and how things like this are normal for me. My friends ask, "How can you function in the world knowing all of this? All these crossovers and the things that you know?" To me it just is because it has to be, because it's part of who I am.

This lifetime is about healing from what's been done to me in past lifetimes. It's not that I obsess over my past lives. I only know about the ones that pertain to things happening in this life, and only when my ancestors feel it's appropriate for me to know, or to my benefit to know. If a memory is not to help me in this life, there's no reason for me to know what happened before. I have had too many previous lifetimes to remember them all at once. That amount of information would be overwhelming for anyone.

Of course, most people don't remember what happened to them before their current life. The veil that comes down when we're born blocks the memory of the other side and of past lives. So why do I remember? Why do some of the young children remember until a certain age? Those of us with this sight remember because, when we chose to come back, we did so with an intentional and wide-open connection to Spirit to help us with our chosen purpose for this life. The veil is allowed to be more transparent for us because this transparency is appropriate to our soul's purpose. For some, this transparency only lasts until certain ages when the purpose of the memories is fulfilled, and for others like me, we have the memories for our entire lives.

Most of the children coming into the world now are coming in more "awake," with a full, strong connection to Spirit. Those that have been recognized as "gifted," who remember past lives, who are clairvoyant or mediums, are the children to whom the world should pay attention. These children are old souls who can handle this deep connection to Spirit and have come back to our world to be our teachers. These children have an excess of energy, in addition to second sight, because this energy is being channeled through them by Spirit. It comes from God. It is important to recognize these children, and any people with true psychic gifts, as teachers, because they are the ones who can guide others who are not ready for such a connection to Spirit to still accomplish their purpose.

I have excess energy as well. I can accomplish much in a day, to the surprise of others. This is my secret: I have an open channel to Spirit that flows through me with great intensity, just like these children. Sometimes it is so very strong that I feel like "superwoman," like I can do anything. Those high points will usually end the next day when I have to crash and take a rest because my human body cannot handle that kind of a charge. Over the years, my body has adapted to handle more and more of this energy, but it took time and training from my guides and angels.

Every relationship that I have ever had in this lifetime has had a connection to a time before. The other person often doesn't remember as much, or anything, from the previous lifetime, yet each of us has a "role" in the "play" that is set up based on that past experience, and this role is imperative for our growth and inner understanding. Many lessons for our soul can only happen through living a human experience, and none of the lives we have lived have been a waste. The irony of this is that there will never be another moment like the moment you're living right now, with the people who currently surround you. This is why the present life is still so precious. Forgiveness and miracles are possible as long as you're alive in this life. We are much more than most of us think we are. We are capable of much more than we give ourselves credit for. When I get out of my own way and remove doubts and fears, my daily life becomes a blur of energy and accomplishments. When Spirit is allowed to flow through us, anyone can accomplish just as much and have similar days. Our free will gives us choices in the moment, but the most important choice is to love with all our heart and to have the courage to experience all life has to offer in this current lifetime. The ability to remember not only helps those who have access to their past lives to accomplish their own purpose, this ability can also be used to help others accomplish their purpose as well. This is why this gift exists, as a tool to help manage the puzzle pieces that make up our souls' evolution.

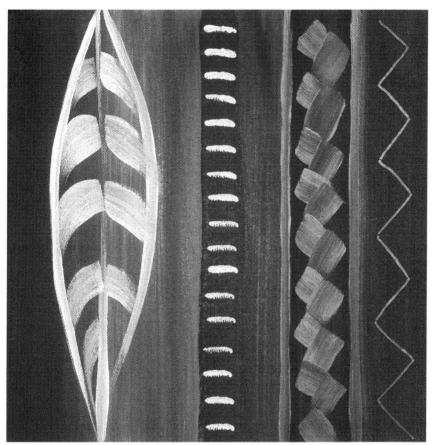

tribal                                                    2012

*No matter how dire the world looks from your perspective, there is always love available for you as an option. It takes courage to find it and to heal from what's been done.*

# little deer

*This story was told to me in 1997 by one of my guides. It was told to me from these two perspectives because they were trying to help me understand that we always have choices that lead either to our happiness and fulfillment or keep us trapped in bad situations. In life, we may stay in a given situation that is not what we desire or we may make the choice to move into another situation that helps us grow, which is what the Creator would want for us in most cases. The issue that most often arises is that we become stuck at a certain point in life and we can't see that we have another choice. People in situations that seem dire often believe there's no other way out because they are afraid of things getting worse; the devil that they know is better than the devil that they don't. But in reality, they're living with the 'devil' in most cases and the scenario that would bring them joy and happiness takes courage and faith to achieve by making a choice for things to be different. Our fear of the unknown is the thing that keeps us from achieving our dreams. This is true for almost all of us. Finding the courage inside of us to move forward usually requires something big happening in our lives to act as a catalyst: a mother seeing her children abused is motivated to leave the abuser because that's her last straw, or a woman breaks up with her boyfriend because he's going too deeply into drugs and she knows she can't help him. These events help force us to make the choice that breaks the hurtful cycle for all involved. In this past-life story that was shared with me about my soul's journey, I did not see the way out at the time, as sad as that is to know now. The two versions of the story, how things were versus how they could have been, were shown to me only when I went to the other side after that lifetime.*

I tell this story, not as the young woman I am now, but as an old woman of a lifetime gone by. I shall speak of the past, how it was and how it could've been. Long ago, there was a girl child born to a Native tribe in the northern woods. This child entered life in the midst of a celebration. The proud parents had a gift of love that was envied throughout the tribe, and this love had produced a beautiful baby. The grand-mother had taken the child to be named, as was the custom. It was not long before she spotted a little deer with its mother. So the child became known as "Little Deer."

The Spirit had blessed Little Deer with inner joy that showed and danced through whatever the child did. Her grandfather was a shaman and suspected his granddaughter had many gifts of the spirit. Little Deer was a talented girl child. She learned very quickly to sew, do beadwork, and paint the teepees with stories. She could create anything the tribe needed, more beautifully and with what seemed to be less effort than any other woman in the tribe. It was as if all the ancestor grand-mothers who had gone before were born within Little Deer. She had the gift of heal-ing within her hands. It was as if Spirit itself guided her hands.

Not knowing she was different from any other girl child, Little Deer did not realize what gifts she possessed. The grandfather started to teach her, when she was very young, how to listen to the words of the animals and understand what they could teach her. She learned to venture into the woods without fear and listen to what the animals might reveal to her. One day, around the age of five summers, Little Deer was out gathering berries when a bear cub arrived at her side and insisted she play with him. Little Deer had not yet learned that where there are bear cubs their mother is not far away.

Little Deer was enjoying the new friendship with the cub, when out of no-where the mother bear appeared in a fury, took one swipe with a claw, and slashed through the flesh of Little Deer's right knee. Before the bear could do any more harm, an arrow that had been shot from the bow of Little Deer's grandfather startled the bear and she and her cub left and disappeared into the forest. Surviving a bear attack was strong medicine, and Little Deer's grandfather realized that his granddaughter was now gifted with bear medicine. This little one was special, so he began to teach the ways of healing and Spirit to her.

Two more summers passed, and then the white men appeared. They talked long and took much. At first the tribe welcomed them, but soon realized that their way of life was threatened. More white men came, and warnings came to the tribe in visions and dreams. Little Deer was haunted by dreams of fire, and her parents would have to comfort her at night.

One day in early spring, Little Deer was with her mother sewing beads onto a doeskin dress when the scouts came running into the village yelling of white men, hundreds of white men, surrounding the tribe. That was the only warning received before their guns started to fire, slaughtering the tribe. Little Deer's grandfather grabbed her and put her inside the hollow of a tree before going back to fight. That was the last time Little Deer saw her grandfather. Through a tiny hole she watched as the teepees were set on fire and her tribe and family killed. She saw her father try to save her mother as their teepee burned but they both became trapped, and Little Deer watched her parents' faces as they perished in the fire.

When the fighting was over and the white men left, Little Deer was the only survivor. She had never heard a silence so complete before that day. The pain in her heart was so overwhelming that she thought she too would now die. But she did not die. She wondered why she had been the only one to survive. She was in shock for a long time. She stayed in the tree and did not move, waiting to see if just one other person might have escaped as well. But no, she was now alone, only seven summers old.

Little Deer had only witnessed the ceremony to release the spirit of a deer before it could nourish the tribe. So she did not know how to perform the ceremony to release the spirits of people, of her family, so that they could move on into the next life unhindered. She talked to them as if they were still there with her, and felt as though her grandfather was helping her. Amongst the ashes she found one of her grandfather's medicine rattles. It was charred but otherwise still intact. She was able to gather a few things that the white men had not taken or destroyed; a knife, deerskin, and a few other items that she packed to take with her. The grandfather's spirit was telling her to leave this place but she did not want to leave until she performed a simple ceremony using her grandfather's medicine rattle to release the spirits. The tears ran down like rivers on her cheeks but it was done at last, as best as she could do for them.

Her bear medicine protected her for many months as she journeyed to find a new tribe. She knew the white men had not wiped out every tribe. She had heard stories of other tribes with more warriors. They could fight the white men. She would warn them, though she wished the warning had come sooner for her tribe. Little Deer was tired and hungry. It was getting increasingly difficult to follow the animal guides, for her spirit became weakened from the loneliness of the loss of her family. It was a lot to bear, and one night as she fell asleep wrapped in a deerskin under a tree, she hoped a warrior would find and rescue her.

Someone did find her but it was not a warrior from another tribe, it was a white trapper who had no use for a seven year old Native girl. But he felt sorry for her and he gave her food and shelter until she got her strength back.

[this is where the story changes from how it was to how it could've been...]

[how it was…]   The Trapper was lonely and thought that at the very least this Native girl could cook and clean for him since she owed him her life. She would have surely died if he had not found her, and this is what he told her over and over again until she also believed it to be true. She lived in a wood shack with the Trapper, and cooked for him and kept the house while he was away hunting.

Little Deer got used to him. He pretty much left her alone, and she pitied him. Little by little, her spirit died. The Trapper treated her like an animal, but at least she had food and shelter. Where else could she go? The Trapper would travel for weeks in one direction without seeing anyone. Surely if he had come across a Native tribe of her people, he would tell her and take her there, she thought. Or she would fantasize that maybe someone else would find her in the middle of these woods and rescue her. Neither of these things happened. The Trapper came and went, barely speaking to her unless telling her to do something. One night when she was 13 summers old, the Trapper stumbled through the door with whiskey on his breath. He kept a barrel of whiskey in the old shed in the back behind the house. He had been gone for a long time, and sometimes Little Deer wondered if he was coming back at all.

He had never come near where she slept until this night. He woke her, telling her she owed him now that she was a woman and no longer a child. She was now to please him in the ways of a wife. Little Deer protested, saying he was too old to be a husband to such a young girl; that he was drunk, and to leave her alone. With that, the Trapper became furious. He threw Little Deer onto the floor, raped and beat her.

She could barely walk the next morning. The shock and pain flooded her spirit for days after. How could he do this? How could she leave? Where would she go? She felt trapped like an animal, even after her bruises healed. Now she was grateful when he left, and she hoped he would not come back. Little Deer remembered the love that was shared between her parents and she knew what he was doing to her was very wrong, but she did not know how or to where she could escape. Her will and spirit were broken, and her strength seemed to be gone.

The more he came at her, the colder she would act to him and the weaker in spirit she became. When she was 18 summers old, she was with child, but he beat her and the child died inside her. She was so disgusted with him that it was as if she would leave her body whenever he came near and touched her, so she would no longer feel. As time went on, the Trapper would drink more and more whiskey and become more and more violent with her.

At the age of 21 summers, in the middle of the winter, the Trapper beat her so badly that she could not get up. He threw her out into the snow and left her with no food or firewood. She could not dry her moccasins by the fire, and she could not get warm. She could not hunt for herself because she was too weak. Her entire body was numb from the cold. She could no longer walk. Later that night, her spirit freed itself from her body, and she was able to escape this life and rejoin her people.

[how it could've been…] The Trapper was lonely and he thought that at the very least this Native girl could cook and clean for him, since she owed him her life. He told her this over and over again, hoping to have it so ingrained in her that she would believe it to be true. Little Deer knew better than that. She remembered all the things that her grandfather taught her. She was grateful to the Trapper but she didn't owe him anything. Little Deer kept her strong will and knew her grandfather's spirit was with her. She would also call on her bear medicine to help her when she needed it. She cooked and cleaned for the Trapper but was grateful when he would go off so she could practice her Native rituals. She grew older and her body stronger. Her animal friends would warn her when he was coming back so she could have things ready for him, so as not to anger him.

When she turned 13 summers, she noticed the Trapper starting to eye her. She felt uneasy, and something inside her told her it was almost time to leave; time to search again for her people. Little Deer had found a hiding place, a hollow between some rocks where she had started to store food and supplies for her future journey. She had been preparing for a long time. She wanted to be ready when Spirit told her it was time to go. She placed everything there that she had brought with her six summers past, including her grandfather's medicine rattle.

Soon after the night of the seventh moon, the Trapper stumbled through the door with whiskey on his breath. He had been celebrating a successful hunt. He had never come near her while she slept until this night. There was a strange look in his eye, and Little Deer could feel the blood pumping through her body. She was strong and not afraid. He started telling her that she owed him her life, that she was no longer a child and was to please him the way a wife pleases a husband. She protested, saying "shame on you, you old drunk man" and telling him to leave her alone. He became furious but was uncoordinated because of the whiskey. He lunged at her, but she bolted out of the shack and ran.

Little Deer was grateful that grandmother moon was shining that night, lighting her way, and she knew it was time. She ran and ran until she reached her hidden place and her hidden stash, with gratitude in her heart to Spirit for having forewarned her to store these things for her journey. The Trapper, too drunk to chase after her, figured she would be back later because she had nowhere to go or any way to survive in these deep woods. But he was wrong and he never saw her again.

Little Deer felt strong for having escaped and outsmarted the Trapper with the help of Spirit. Spirit did not let her down. She was guided North, beyond the Trapper's territory. She let the animals guide her, and felt her grandfather's presence. She traveled until the time of the ninth moon. She was starting to get low on food and supplies, and she could feel the weather changing to fall. Her spirit was strong but her body was tired, and she started to get weary and discouraged. Maybe all the tribes had traveled further north to get away from the white men and she might not find her people. Yet, just as she had that thought, an eagle flew overhead. Seeing that eagle lifted her spirit and gave her the strength to keep going.

A few short days later, she found a stream and was drinking from it when she looked up and over the landscape to see teepees similar to those used by her people. She got up, mesmerized as if in a trance, and walked until she got to the center of the village and stood there. She was processing all kinds of feelings inside of herself, amazed and in deep gratitude at where the spirits had taken her. An old woman walked up to her and gently said, "We had a vision of you coming and we are glad you are here." Little Deer was so overwhelmed with joy she couldn't speak. She had found her people, never to be separated again. She shared her story with those around her, and they knew she was a special one, one that could hear the spirits. She helped these people in many ways over the years. She fell in love with a strong, goodhearted warrior and had many children. She grew old with her heart full of love and happiness. She had found her home.

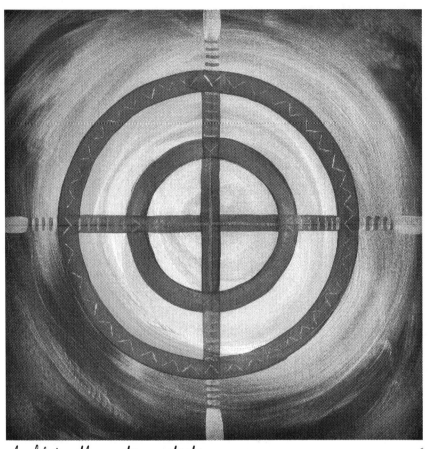

shield for the water protectors                    2016

*My angels and guides, be with me through this process.*
*Guide my words, thoughts, and deeds, this day and every day*
*as I follow my path and strive to fulfill my purpose. Aho*

## walking in two worlds

Over the years I have remembered all the big signs from Spirit as if they were traffic signs along a road. These larger, more direct messages and experiences from the unseen world got my attention and corrected my trajectory when I was otherwise unable to turn away from a bad path in my unconscious state. I now have what I call "a sacred practice" that has strengthened my faith, helped me to grow, and helps me to become more committed to myself and my path every day. I have found that being in the natural world and connecting to our Mother Earth adds indescribable gifts to my day to day life. It has taught me to truly "listen" from a different place. If I take a walk in the woods in the morning or do ceremony, and ask for Spirit's help, I receive it. When I became "aware" and started to walk through my life with my eyes, ears, and heart open, everything started to change for me. A subtle shift started to happen, of which I wasn't initially aware. Conversations with others started to have a deeper feel to them, coming from a place of love and compassion. I found myself in a grounded, centered place, unlike earlier in my life.

I started learning to use my gifts by paying attention to my dreams. Once I started down this path, I would have moments when I would get a "download" or "channel" from Spirit. This happened for the first time one morning when I woke in my bedroom in Maine and Spirit gave me a prayer to recite. This prayer came to me in 1998. It was given to me as a gift from my angels and guides to help me along my journey. I have said this prayer every day since. I share it with you now, as my gift to you on your journey.

*My Creator, My God —*
*Please guide my spirit through this day — That I may live my truth, hold my pow-*
*er & integrity. That I may be thankful for this time of learning, this incubation*
*period for my love, my creativity, and myself.*
*Please help me to be patient, accepting of this time and to recognize and acknowl-*
*edge the messages and the gifts that you constantly send me to sustain my spirit.*
*Amen, Aho!*

My friends who know about my gifts have asked me how I can walk in two worlds. They don't just mean living in the two worlds of my present life and the memories of those lives from before, but also how I went from growing up in an Italian Catholic environment to now being so involved in Native ceremonies, seemingly two separate spiritual worlds. My only answer is that ancestors from both lineages have come together on parallel paths to further my spiritual understanding. If they were not doing this, why then would Jesus have appeared in that room to the priest and I, and guided me to my Native grandfather? I needed to have that very specific, literal experience as validation of this truth so I could recognize it in my human form. I question myself like anyone does. Every time that I do, they remind me that Jesus came to me in this life three times. Those visitations were a gift so that I would not question what was being asked of me or what I was supposed to do. My ancestors tell me that I am a bridge for the purpose of healing what has been done between not only the White and Native people, but all peoples.

My spirit grandfather has told me that if the Europeans had arrived at our shores without their guns and energies of violence, then we would all be living in a totally different world now. Turtle Island was supposed to be a sanctuary. There were ways that we could have blended and lived together. However, that could not be when the Europeans viewed Natives with hostility and fear, and came here with greed in their hearts, looking to take and steal whatever was to their benefit. When you believe another people are less than you, lessons need to be learned, for we are all equal. Even now there is such a disconnect between the races, and we all have our stories of persecution. The same healing that is needed for one is needed for all. Any victimizing or controlling energies need to be cleared from our lives and our earth. Violence destroys sacred vision.

I attended a Catholic service on the reserve in Canada a few years ago as part of the funeral for a baby who was taken too soon from my Native brother and his family. We, my Native brothers and sisters, were asked to come to the service to drum and sing prayer songs for the family. I was a bit self-conscious being in a Catholic church with my Native brothers and sisters. I had tears in my eyes when I heard the prayers and the "Our father" said in our Mi'Kmaq language. I have been trying to learn our language ever since I started coming to Canada. I've learned a word or two here and there. I still cannot speak it but my comprehension of what's being discussed when it's spoken between others is coming along a little at a time. But even with these limitations to my understanding of the service, I was incredibly moved to see another group of people embracing the Native and Christian spiritual paths together, as I had been doing throughout my life. It was a sign of how we could overcome the differences between Europeans and Native people.

I really struggled when I was younger. I always felt there were a lot of missing pieces to my puzzle. And I was right. The missing pieces were residual trauma and experiences from my previous lifetimes. As a young person, this was not something I realized was possible. I was raised Catholic, and they don't believe in past lives so I didn't either, until my ancestors revealed them to me and I started to remember. This is when the pieces of my puzzle started to click into place. Why did I fall into that abusive relationship? Why did I break up with that boyfriend? Why did I make those choices? You see, none of it made sense to me. I didn't make sense to myself. Eventually, these past life memories would all be revealed to me one at a time, as I grew enough to handle them. It would take thirty years for me to start to make sense of most of what I experienced.

It took this long so that I could handle the information emotionally, mentally, and sometimes physically, because our mind and our body and our spirit are all connected. We are also connected to our "tribe." The tribe with which we are reincarnated over and over. These can be people we love, those we have a contract with, those we have karmic ties with, or people who just really love us on the soul level and enter lifetimes with us to help us push past our comfort zone so that we can grow. My spirit grandfather tells me that none of us are ever done learning. This came up one day when I was with my cousin, Wyn. She and I were struggling with some similar issues in our lives, and in conversation we both threw up our hands and said, "Are we done yet?!" Grandfather said to me, with a laugh, "Done? We are never done learning. None of us are ever done learning, not on this side or that side."

I have never had children in this life. Other than my first boyfriend, Jonah, all the other men in my life would not have made suitable fathers. I knew that for sure with Zac, and after I made the decision to not have our baby, I knew I would not have children after that. Aside from this insight, I have since learned that the nightmares and visions that made no sense to me as a child were memories of past lives. These memories were particularly violent and frightening because they all took place during the occupation of the Americas, during which I had many lifetimes. These lifetimes are the most recent, and therefore the freshest in my soul's memory. They also held the karmic ties that were the additional reason I could not emotionally cope with having children in this lifetime.

In one of these past lives, I remember that I was preparing food when many soldiers came into the village on horseback, yelling. They ran their horses in between the villagers, and I felt panic run through me as I tried to see where my children were. I had two children; a boy about six years old and a little girl of three years old. We had adapted and lived among the whites in relative peace for a while now. We lived in separate villages, but peacefully coexisted without much contact. We had adapted the best we could to these new ways of living. Now, the soldiers were forcing us on either side of a line and would not let us cross. I started to scream because my children were on the other side of the line. I tried explaining to the soldier in front of me but he didn't understand our language. Then, in panic and desperation, I fought to get to my children. I started to push past the soldiers but it was no use. They were not letting me through and they didn't understand or care that I was telling them that they were separating me from my children. We had become a broken people, and as I looked across to the other side of the line, I knew there wasn't anyone there who would care for them. So I kept fighting to cross the barrier that the soldiers created as they were rounding us up like cattle. I later learned that I was Cherokee in this memory, and this was the start of what would be called the Trail of Tears. The soldiers were moving us out of our homes and were taking us far away from the land of our ancestors. We were on foot for many, many weeks and months. Many of us died. I never saw my children again. My spirit grandfather told me that my boy ran into the hills and got away when the soldiers came, but I never knew what happened to him after that. My little girl died of hunger and cold while laying by a fire, because there was no one to care for her. This little girl was reborn with me again into my current family, but not as my child this time.

In another memory from a different life, my people had set up our teepees in a wooded area by a creek. We were going about our daily tasks when screaming started at the edge of the encampment, followed by chaos and confusion. I had been holding the little girl I was caring for as I did my chores. She was about two years old and was my sister's child. She was the last living relative from my family, all of the rest of whom were lost in previous attacks. I remember the river turned red with blood, as the soldiers showed no mercy. They surprised us because we believed we were at a truce. They had made their way into camp without warning because people were not initially alarmed at the sight of them. When we all heard the first screams, and I saw that they had started killing us, I ran with the baby. I only made it a short way before a soldier with blond hair grabbed her out of my arms and smashed her head against a tree and killed her. I collapsed in grief, screaming. I wanted to die too, but for some reason they did not kill me. The remaining tribe members who fled had to drag me away across the ground because I was so distraught over the loss of the baby. A big part of me, of my soul, was broken in that moment. My soul screamed out in a pain so deep that it would be many lifetimes before I could have faith again. The shock of what was happening to my people, along with the loss of my last family member, was too overwhelming. My people had lived in peace for so many years before the white ones came to our shores. This kind of evil had not touched us in generations, but then the white devils came, and came, and came.

In my very next lifetime, when I was around six years old, I would play at a stream, and there was a little white girl who played with me there. This was during the era when Native children were being taken away from their people to be raised as White in boarding schools. We continued to play together as we grew, and when we became adults I still thought she was my friend. When I got pregnant and was ready to give birth, because this friend was with me, I felt safe having my baby in a White hospital. After the hard work of labor, I had little choice but to close my eyes and sleep and rest. When I woke I found both my baby and my White friend missing. I asked the hospital staff where they were and they told me they would both be right back, but I never saw my friend or my baby again. She had betrayed me and stolen my baby so she could be raised "civilized." This woman truly believed she was doing what was best because it was what the priest had told her. I don't know if my baby ended up with a White family or in residential school. I never knew what happened to her, and I hated this woman for the rest of my life for her betrayal of me.

In my present life, this woman, Anne, returned to a lifetime with me as a close relative, to force us both to work through the karma of what she had done to me then. My hate for her was strong, even as children. I never understood why. I thought it was a problem with me and that I was just mean. I tried to "be nice" but I really avoided her as much as I could. It wasn't until Anne needed me to help save her children that I connected with her in a different way. When her youngest was born, I went to the hospital to see the baby out of obligation. I say obligation because I had built an emotional wall between us over the years, and I told myself I was not going to get attached.

As I entered the hospital room, I immediately stopped in my tracks, overwhelmed by the presence of a spirit in the back left corner, opposite from where Anne lay in bed with her new baby girl. It was an old and very wise Asian guide. I immediately heard him start to speak to me in a demanding tone as I stood there in shock. He said for me to tell her that she had to "earn this baby" or she would not be able to keep her. If she did not "earn her," he would take her back. He had not wanted the baby girl to come down yet, but her soul had insisted. He continued, saying that this soul was coming in to save her older sister, so he was giving Anne a chance to fight to keep the gift of this baby.

Anne's situation in life at this time and her choices that led to it, as well as her past lives, had now put her child at risk. Her karma from taking another's child in our past lifetime was now confronted by my need to find the strength to overcome my feelings towards her. We needed to work together to overcome these influences and save her children. This situation healed a lot of the hurt she had caused me, and she also had to accept my help and be humbled for what she did.

Through an immense health struggle in the youngest child's early life, and through my willingness to help her save her children and keep them safe, we healed some of our karma from what had happened between us before. Anne had no knowledge of the previous lifetime we shared, and her confusion over the nature of our relationship all these years has been hard for her. I have since told Anne what my grandfather revealed to me, and that it took many years of work with Jayne to heal the soul trauma carried from this lifetime alone.

Through my healing process, I received an understanding of much of what I had endured in my earlier years. I was told that this hatred that I carried was why I needed to come into a partially white family in this lifetime, and to even blend in and look white, so that I could get over the hate that I carried in my soul. Whenever you have hate for another race you will inevitably be reincarnated as that race. This is how it is. This is why you need to overcome any discrimination or hate for others. This is why forgiveness is so important. There is a strong possibility that you will be reborn into a family, race, or situation that you had judged harshly before. This is why Jesus taught that you should love your neighbor as yourself, because if you cannot do that in life, there is a chance you will be taught to walk in that person's shoes by living in them in the next life.

These were hard memories for me to write about. I have a hard time reliving what happened, even from where I am now. It still feels like each of these memories happened to me yesterday. My sister, Mary, asked me why I feel so connected to our Native ancestry while she does not. Mary has not had as many lifetimes as a red soul. This may be her first lifetime having any Native blood, so how could she understand my connection? We don't share the same gifts and she doesn't have my soul's memories. She says she only feels Italian. Whenever she talks about this, her voice rises in annoyance because, despite being sisters raised side by side, she and I feel so differently in this regard. Mary always becomes very boisterous when she's frustrated, and once, during a discussion about this, she started to get loud. Mary's son, who was in the other room, laughed and shouted, "Mom, you're the Italian cook of the family and 'Aunty' is the Native American artist. What don't you understand?!" When we heard it put so simply, we both laughed.

As hard as my journey has been for me, it has also been pretty difficult for my family. It has been difficult for them to understand. You can never fully understand another person, because every person alive today has had their own unique journey of many lifetimes.

Every soul has its own purpose and is at a different level from any other, depending on the lifetimes needed to attain its purpose. You may be a young soul seeing life through new eyes, happy and enjoying a simple life or already learning the hard lessons of "cause and effect" from naive choices. You could be an adolescent soul. Most often, souls at this stage would be the ones that we see in places of power or politics, who think that they can control their environments or even control the world. These are the souls that are like teenagers who haven't yet learned. Then there are the older souls who are at various levels, from young adult to the very old, wise ones who have reached higher levels of knowledge based on their experiences. In this way, the stages of life reflect the stages of the soul's journey on the other side. Can you judge one stage of a person's life as better than any other? No. Just because a teenager can be frustrating and foolish, does not mean they are not just as worthy of respect as a person who is older and wiser. The older and wiser person also had to be a teenager and learn and grow to get where they are. Be careful when you judge others, for they are just in a different stage of learning than you. No one is better than another and everyone is very special in their own way. Every soul has a purpose that is unlike any other soul's. People in your life could be there to wreak havoc so that you develop the strength to push through darkness, or they could be there to love you so deeply that it brings you to tears and you acquire the ability to love and have faith. We are all here together in this singular time to fulfill Creator's vision.

Often our emotions are a guidepost to what is truly broken in us. When we repress our emotions it can manifest in our bodies as illness. The deeper the emotional trauma is, the more significant the disease. People in the medical field are just now finally opening back up to the way Native healers have healed for many hundreds of years. The mind, body, spirit connection is not a "New Age" concept, it is an ancient knowing of who we all are and who we have always been. Your mind, body, and spirit make you whole.

Because a soul's evolution is both a personal and interconnected experience, there is no avoiding challenge in life, either personally or on a global and societal scale. For an individual soul to grow, or for all of our souls to grow as a collective people, we have to go through dark times and challenges and make it to the other side to develop clarity and healing. This is not an easy task. It takes a lot of courage and faith, both of which are lacking in the society we live in now. However, this does not mean things are hopeless for all people. A lot of the things we are dealing with in our world now are a reflection of the collective, and they are happening so that we will once again find our faith. We will once again find connection to the unseen world.

When the horrible genocide happened to my people it took our numbers on this continent from approximately 60 million to 800,000 in just a few short years. None of us, neither the perpetrators nor the victims, can move on from that trauma if it is ignored and repressed. This genocide has been lied about in history books to cover up much of what really happened, and to make it seem as though we have moved on from the prejudice and violence that caused it. But it can't be covered up for those of us who remember, or for those who are still living under oppression because they are Native. If this trauma is not acknowledged and healed by everyone as a society, then just as an individual develops an illness from repressed emotion, we can develop a sickness as a society that leads to more prejudice, hate, and trauma. Societal trauma and discord are a direct result of ignorance of the natural order of life, and of ignorance of the need for balance and healing to recover from trauma in order to rise above prejudice and violence.

Collectively, we are all here to heal what we have all done to each other out of ignorance. The dream is that we will get past the stages of humanity that have violence, prejudice, hate, and greed, and the next generations will be able to live without them. We live in a world of abundance, but we also live in a world where our true nature is hidden from us. If each of us lived our life's purpose without fear, we would already live in a different world than what we see in front of us today. This is why walking in two worlds is so important. It is also how my ability to do so, both with past and present lives and with Christian and Native spirituality, can serve as an example for how we all can overcome our hurt, hatred, and prejudice to move forward as one people. I was not able to do this without much learning and experience in this life, all with the guidance of others. It took time to learn how the pieces of my past life puzzle fit with this one, and it took time to learn to balance my Native and Italian ancestry and spirituality. It took time to balance and heal past trauma that stood between me and current people in my life. But this balance is what everyone is striving for in their individual soul's purpose, and what we all must strive for collectively, in order to understand each other and come together. This is why I am the bridge who walks in two worlds, because I, along with others like me, must teach that we all walk in all worlds.

spirit horse                                      2012

*While alone at the beach one day, my spirit grandfather, spirit grandmother, and Mark showed up to walk with me. My grandfather said, "You are supported by those of us on the other side. You have been continually supported and will continue to be so. You do not go through these things alone. There is much for you to remember. It will come in time."*

## my spirit brother & the unseen

My understanding of my brother Mark, the Native man with the striking blue eyes who I had seen at the fair as a child, developed while I was struggling in my second marriage. I had gone to see Jayne to get help with some of these marital issues, but Mark's story came through unexpectedly instead. At the start of this visit, I told Jayne that I had been having a particularly strong feeling that there was someone with me in spirit, and it turned out to be Mark. When Mark had died, his new perspective from the other side of the veil allowed him to recognize that I was his sister from our shared prior lifetime, and so his spirit had been drawn to mine. In our current lifetime he was just about thirteen years older than me, so he'd been with me many years, waiting for me to grow up so I could help him. He told me that my spirit was much stronger than his and that he was proud of me. He asked me to help him on the other side and I said I would.

In this life, Mark grew up somewhere in Montana and he had three brothers. The details he gave me were somewhat vague, but from what I understand the four of them were Native American but were adopted by a White family and given Christian names when they were between six and ten years old. I sensed there was some confusion around this for them, because they had initially grown up with their birth family in the traditional ways, and then that abruptly ended as they were taken out of that environment and forced into residential schools and adopted. I don't know what happened to his parents but he told me they died sometime after he and his siblings were taken away. Though they had all been raised in the Native ways early in life, the children were all half-blooded, and in Mark this was apparent with his striking blue eyes. He and his brothers had a tough time growing up away from their people. When Mark was eighteen he was drafted and had fought in Vietnam. He was heavily traumatized by that war, as most of the soldiers were. The soldiers played a lot of cards during downtime, and some significance was given to the expression "luck of the draw," not just in terms of card games but also in terms of who made it out alive. Mark got a Jack of Spades tattooed on the back of his shoulder, and after that the guys in Vietnam nicknamed him Jack. From what he tells me, there was a close camaraderie between the soldiers in his unit, and it was pure chance which of them survived. Between experiencing the horrors of that war and losing men he had developed a close bond with, he came back to the U.S. suffering from Post-Traumatic Stress Disorder, although this diagnosis was not recognized at the time. Because of the local political opposition to the war, none of the returning soldiers were treated as heroes or warriors. In fact it was often the opposite, and Mark felt lost upon returning home to this reception while carrying the trauma of war and lost friends on his back.

It was only shortly after this that I encountered him at the fair when I was ten years old. Even in spirit he still remembered the connection we made when we saw each other, and he had been shocked by it too. He had been very troubled at that time and had been traveling on his motorcycle, running away from his memories of what happened overseas. He told me that shortly after our encounter he traveled back out West into the desert, and was drinking heavily. He was killed in a bar fight in the desert on a sunny day. As he lay face-down, dying in the sand, he thought to himself, "what a wasted life this one was."

After Jayne's help with filling in details, I called around to many different Native motorcycle groups in Montana to try to find anyone who had known him. I had no luck finding his family or his brothers with the little information I had. I have recently found out that my Blackfoot family lineage has a possible connection with him in Montana. I believe Mark and his brothers were part of the same Blackfoot band as my family, which is our possible blood connection in this life. Many years later I was told by the ancestors that, had he not died, we would've met each other again in this life and the family connection would've come full circle.

Once I understood who Mark was to me, it opened communication between us and he assisted me in my life, sometimes daily. I could "feel" him near me. I continued to see Jayne and discuss the things I was picking up on to make sure I was not missing anything in this communication with Mark. I was learning how to "hear" more clearly through this continual interaction. Mark taught me many things because he shared an understanding of what happens on the other side of the veil.

Finally the time came when Mark was ready and asked if I would help him to transition and cross over. I performed a private ceremony for him in the woods by a stream behind my house. I built a fire and followed my spirit grandfather's specific instructions. I would have had no idea how to do this otherwise, but I managed to stay in the moment, listen, and help Mark make the journey to the next world. Our ancestors were with us, and Mark's transition was completed that night.

Shortly thereafter, I got a call from Jayne. She asked if I would come with her to help energetically clear a property. She said that there was a Native connection to the land there and she would need my help, so I agreed to go. I wanted to help, and I knew it would also be practice for me to use these new skills I had been working on. This would be my first introduction to a tribe of people I had never heard of. They were called "the Forresters" or "the Tree People."

When Jayne and I arrived at the property to begin clearing it, we sat under a tree to perform the ceremony. Even with all that Mark had taught me I was still not fully accustomed to this, and I was a bit overwhelmed by the feelings that were cascading from this area into me. I followed Jayne's lead through the clearing and healing ritual she was doing, and I kept quiet for most of it. She then said, "It is done." I told her I wasn't feeling right, so we went back to her office and I sat down. As soon as I sat, my throat became so tight it felt like it was closing up. Jayne told me to relax and just let whatever it was flow through.

A spirit had been trying to speak to me, and as soon as I opened myself to it he immediately got my attention and addressed me. He called himself "Sesca of the Tree People." He wanted to tell me his story, and said he had been murdered by the Europeans when they first came over to this continent. Sesca told me that the Tree People were a band of physically small people because they were half human and half fairy. They were a special and magical people who lived in harmony with the land and animals along the entire East Coast of this Turtle Island.

At this point my throat became so tight that Jayne took over and got the rest of the history. Sesca continued by saying that all the other Native American tribes along the coast, from what is now Florida to Canada, had protected and revered these people and never warred with them. The Tree People had never been a witness to violence. They were the keepers and planters of the forest, and had many special gifts with which to do so. Like fairies, their job was to take care of the earth. The Forresters were the ones who would plant certain trees and plants in such a way and in certain combinations that they would create good homes for the particular animals that they wanted to attract to that area. They had these special gifts granted to them by the fairy realm because they were related. The women of the tribe were healers and knew the uses of the plants for medicinal and culinary purposes.

I was forever changed after hearing of these people. Some memory of working with them as a healer in another time long ago was triggered in me, but it is not clear enough for me to know the whole story. Yet, between this memory and Sesca's description, I have a clear image of these people, all of whom were smaller in stature, had large eyes, high cheekbones, slightly pointed ears, hollow bones like birds, and were extremely light. They looked completely different from any other Natives. Their homes were domed and made of Willow and Birch in the winter and of reeds in the summer.

When Sesca spoke to me again, after Jayne had helped me to channel and I had recovered, I could "see" his face. He told me that he was the one in the tribe who had been responsible for communicating with the white birch tree spirit. He told me that his race were an innocent people when the white man came. They had no weapons or fear, for they lived in harmony with all. The white men killed his two-year-old daughter and his wife right in front of him, unprovoked and for no reason. His son tried to run away and was captured and killed as well. From there, the entire band was murdered. After recounting this, he then said, "Violence is a poison that has run rampant on this earth. Harmony has been destroyed. We have much to learn."

When the channel was over it took me days and weeks to integrate all the emotions and information I had learned about Sesca and his people. I could find no written accounts of them in my search for more information. Grandfather told me there were many verbal stories and legends of the Tree People, and sometimes they are confused with the stories of the "little people." The stories of the Little People are slightly different, but common to most North American tribes. It was an unexpected and shocking experience to learn of a people so unexpectedly different and magical but who there is no physical record of. That was the first major experience I had after Mark had gone where I was able to use skills he had helped teach me.

Mark taught me many things about the unseen world. He told me that when souls cross over they are immediately granted clarity, and this reveals their mission or purpose in life. Those that commit suicide or die tragically of their own accord learn of the contracts they held with other souls and the beautiful lives that they could have led. In those instances, they always wish they had not made the final choices that they did. Most feel sorry immediately for taking their own lives because of the hurt they have caused others by doing so, and they mourn their unfulfilled lives. Upon seeing the larger perspective of their lives and what was to be but is now never possible, most of them want to undo that last act and jump back into their bodies. Of course this cannot be, and they realize it's too late for them to fulfill the roles they would have played in others' lives, thus fulfilling their purpose. The relief from pressures and pain that a person seeks by committing suicide can never happen for them on the other side. There can be no relief from the things we face in life because we have chosen them for ourselves as the lessons we undertake for our soul's evolution. Mark explained that we have to work through them. In order to continue to grow on a spiritual level, any souls who pass from suicide or from accidental but self-destructive choices still have to fulfill their contracts, only now with people who cannot hear or see them. It is a struggle for these souls to do this, and if they fail, they have to repeat the same pressures and pain in the next life. From what Mark told me, this can then become a recurring struggle in the next life that the soul must overcome in order to move on through that life lesson. This is part of the spiritual principle which states that what you put out into the world will always return to you. This is called "cause and effect," and I pray that a basic understanding of this natural law comes to more people so that they don't make self-destructive choices and can fulfill their purpose. Mark was eventually able to help me, and I was able to help him, but we are still missing the connection between our families and other things that might have been accomplished if Mark had not died from self-destructive choices. He then had to wait for me for years before his soul could move on, when his soul's evolution could have happened faster otherwise. The gift of life is an opportunity to heal, to forgive, and to move forward on your soul's journey. The present moment is when miracles of healing are possible. Difficult relationships and situations are really openings and opportunities for healing on a soul level. The harder they are the deeper the possibilities are for a potential miracle or karmic healing.

on the horizon                                        2005

*The spirits told me this day that what they ask of me is big. Because of this, they will continue to send me signs so that I'll know I'm on the correct path. And at times, they will send me big signs because the tasks at hand will be big. They know I need encouragement and they do this out of love.*

# big signs

A dark cloud descended on my life at the end of my second marriage. My karmic tie to Anne and her circumstances had put me through a living hell. She had gotten herself entangled in an abusive relationship and her children were being hurt, including the little baby girl she had been told she had to "earn the right to keep." During that experience I went through a loss of faith. I searched out our deepest healing ceremonies and traveled to Canada so I could go and pray for her two little girls. In the healing spaces of those ceremonies I offered my tobacco with prayers for their safety, and I promised the spirits that if they saved these girls from the situation they were in then I would, in exchange, commit to participating in the ceremony instead of just coming to witness it and pray. I had no idea what that meant or what to expect moving forward, but my life was about change in a dramatic way after making that promise.

From the very first moment the drums started beating at the first ceremony I attended, and I stepped onto those sacred grounds, I was instructed. I came to pray for Anne's girls. I never expected a transformation of my life in the process, since I wasn't there for myself. My Spirit grandfather went inside me and taught me a way to dance that would give energy to those participating who needed it. He was relentless with me and I was not allowed to rest because those giving of themselves in the ceremony could not rest, and I was there to help them. My Spirit grandfather said to me, "I will teach you this dance, but you are only to do this dance here and in energetic support of the ceremony dancers." While he took control of my body and showed me the dance, I was a bit uncomfortable because it was a very lively dance. All those around me who were also dancing in support of those in the ceremony were kind of just shuffling their feet to conserve their energy for the days ahead, and

I felt like I stood out being so much more active. I did stand out, but I danced the dance anyway in spite of that. Everyone there just thought I was a good dancer. They couldn't believe the energy that I had to keep up this dance for the whole four days of the ceremony. They thought for sure I would tire out and stop. But I did not, I could not. I was sending energy to those who needed it badly, and supporting them even when my feet and my legs ached in pain. I would take breaks in between the songs, as everybody did, but that was it. My ancestors gave me the energy I needed and told me they were channeling that energy through me, down into the earth, and then to those in the ceremony who were carrying all our prayers. Over the next twelve years I attended the ceremony every year that I was able. Each time I did my dance in support of the ceremony dancers. Coming to these ceremonies has set me on the road to my destiny. A destiny I never envisioned.

Also during that first year of ceremony, there was a night dance which was completely dark. No lights were used to assist the dancers or supporters, and I couldn't see anything during the dance. When the dance was over and I started to walk back to my tent, I was walking out of the area when I saw an exceptional man, or at least someone I thought was a physical man. He was at the south exit, standing right next to the door. He was very tall and albino, wearing jeans and a jean jacket. Our eyes met and I had a strange feeling about him that wouldn't leave me. At that moment, I simply thought to myself, "Oh. He's albino and he cannot come to the ceremonies during the day and be in the sun for so long, so he came to the night dance." All of this was just the beginning.

For many years after this first dance, I would go to stand on the outside of the circle to support those who participated. They were the ones who went deeper and sacrificed part of themselves so that Creator would hear their prayers and the prayers they carried for the rest of us. Each year of ceremony I would see and hear things that others did not. I would dance my own dance in support of those carrying the prayers because this is what I had been told to do by Spirit.

Then one of the original leaders of the ceremony passed away. She was a very strong woman and a very strong leader. From the moment I met her she had always accepted me and called me into the inner circle when appropriate. I had even visited her at her home and gotten to know her outside of ceremony, briefly, before Creator called her back to him. The night that she died she appeared at the bottom of my bed. I didn't know she had died until that moment. I was shocked to see her and I did not understand what that meant.

At ceremony a few years after that, I had a vision so strong that I knew in no uncertain terms what was to be asked of me by the ancestors. I was reminded of the promise I had made in exchange for the protection of the girls. The ancestors told me that they were protected and that my prayers had been answered. All the prayers that I offered year after year at this ceremony were not in vain, and now they were going to ask something of me.

This vision came early in the morning. I had settled into my normal rhythm of dancing and watching the ceremony when I realized I was surrounded by a foggy white light. I had a couple of dear friends that were dancing on either side of me but neither of them saw what I saw. And yet, as I witnessed this vision I knew they were supporting me through it even though they could not see what I could.

As soon as the white light appeared, the ceremony leader who had appeared at the bottom of my bed also appeared right in front of me, and I heard her speak to me in a strong tone. It was a very clear message and I understood. After I saw her, another guide appeared to me. He was all white, an albino with long, white hair, the same man I had seen during the night dance that very first time I set foot on those grounds twelve years earlier. Whether he had been living then or not, now he was here in spirit form and he called himself the White Raven.

Then there was a flurry of motion as all of my departed friends and family from this life emerged out of the light, all smiling at me. My Italian grandmother even appeared, looking around and shaking her head and saying, "I do not understand any of this, but I always knew you were special!" I even laughed at the time, because I could never have imagined seeing her spirit at a Native American ceremony. Maybe I could have imagined her showing up in a mass at Church, but not there. That was part of how I knew I was witnessing a true vision.

As my departed family finished visiting with me, my focus was drawn upwards and I saw Jesus there. He tipped his chin at the people in ceremony who were offering prayers and he said, "They understand." Then he tipped his chin to me and he said, "You understand." In that moment I was confused, so I said, "What do I understand?" Jesus responded: "You understand my sacrifice for others." When he said this to me I collapsed out of the vision, and my two friends dancing on either side of me caught me so I did not fall to the ground. I was in shock and shaking, for now I knew what was being asked of me. It was what Creator wanted of me. All that was left was for me to accept it.

The following year, I began to participate in the ceremonies myself. This was my destiny. This is what I'd come here to do. After I had grown to accept this, my spirit grandfather appeared to me one day. He laughed at me, and said, "You really think this is it? You really think this is all we ask of you?" He just continued to laugh in a loving and humorous way and then he was gone.

the wild horse                                            2007

*July 31, 2008. I had a dream that Jonah came back to me after all these years. I knew it was a sign. I had somehow healed all that had happened to me and finally a true love was on the horizon.*

# love

A
s I ride behind Damon on our Harley on a beautiful and warm summer day, surrounded by all of our friends riding along with us, I can smell the sweet scent of the catalpa trees in bloom and I am amazed and grateful for this and every moment of my life. I have a sense of understanding that, for my soul's journey, this is how it had to be and I have made it through to the other side.

Damon was a mechanic and he owned the garage one street over from where I lived. After my second divorce, I needed to find somebody to work on my van, and he was recommended to me by a neighbor. Manny, my latest ex-husband, was very concerned that I was going to get taken advantage of when the van first started having trouble, so he came to check out my van when the brakes started to have problems. Manny looked at my brakes and told me I only needed one new brake pad. "Don't let anybody tell you otherwise," he said. I went and purchased the brake pads myself at an auto parts store, then went to the garage on the next street that my neighbor had recommended.

The first time I met Damon was the moment I walked into his garage and announced that I needed one brake pad done and that the part was in the van. He laughed when I said that, said "Okay," and fixed one brake pad. Now if you're a mechanic, you know never to fix just one brake pad at a time. You always replace them in pairs. But I was so determined that he humored me.

After that first meeting, I would have Damon look at the van every year to make sure everything was running properly in preparation for my long drive to Canada for ceremonies. He was always completely honest and upfront, and I always felt comfortable with him. I started taking my van there exclusively whenever I needed work done. My mom happened to be visiting the second time I took my van to Damon for inspection before the long drive to ceremonies in Canada. When his inspection was done, she took me over to pick up the van and met him. While we were there, Damon said to me, in front of my mother, that if I had any problems on the way up to Canada that I could give him a call and he would come right up to take care of it. I thought the offer was very nice, but I didn't think anything more of it and just said thank you. After we left, my mom pulled me aside and said, "Marie, I think Damon is sweet on you!" Surprised, I replied, "Damon? No, Mom. He is just my friend." She rolled her eyes at me and said, "All right, if you say so." But then she laughed and walked away.

At this point in my life I had decided I wasn't dating anymore. I had had another short relationship with someone after Manny, and it ended, yet again, with a man being a leech on my energy and my finances. The last thing I wanted was another relationship. In my mind that meant there would be no more dating for me, and that was that.

The next year I went back to Damon's garage to get a registration sticker, and for him to check the van over once again for the trip to Canada. While I was there I became distracted at some point, just looking at something, when suddenly Damon was behind me, holding out a single Black-Eyed Susan. He said, "Will you be my girlfriend?" Damon is a bit of a jokester and I was caught completely off guard, slightly unsure if he was serious or not. Also, not having a good history with men and having so many who had taken financial advantage of me, my attempt at a joke in response caught us both by surprise. I laughed, turned to him and said, "I am not buying dinner, Damon!" I didn't mean it to sound so abrupt or callous, and certainly I didn't think Damon was another leech, but it just popped out of my mouth that way. Not even phased, he replied, "Oh, I'll buy dinner!" We both laughed. I made an appointment to come back to get an oil change and I left the garage and went home. I really thought he was just teasing me and joking around. I didn't take Damon seriously at all.

When I went back a few days later for the oil change, Damon asked again, and I realized he seriously wanted to ask me on a date. I was still unsure about dating at all, so in an attempt to thwart his efforts, I decided to just throw everything out there and said, "Okay, Damon. You want a date with me? How do you feel about spirits?" I was convinced at this point in my life that men could not handle my gifts, and I figured that if I just told him about them he would be either intimidated or skeptical and would leave me alone. I did not get the answer I was expecting. Damon looked at me and said, "Oh, they are real! I've seen them!" He then proceeded to tell me his stories. Once when he was a young man, he told me, he was babysitting when he saw an unexplained orb go down a hallway. Then he told me that after his mother died he had cleaned out all of her old Tupperware from the kitchen, and in the middle of the night all the cabinet doors in the kitchen slammed shut, scaring him and his dog. He said he knew it must have been her, upset with him for getting rid of her Tupperware. Surprised, all I could say was, "Really?" Even though I liked his openness, I still wasn't sure I wanted the attention. I thought, *"What can I say now to deflect his interest in me?"* So I continued, "What if I told you I could hear spirits, and I can speak to them. Would you think I was crazy?" He said, "Not at all." I gave in at that point. "Okay, Damon. We can go on a date when I get back from Canada." I went home to pack and I left for Canada the following day.

The ceremonies that year were very powerful. I was fully present, and really wasn't thinking about anything else. I hadn't even thought about Damon the entire time I was there, until a funny thing happened the morning I was leaving to drive home. I felt an unexpected excitement and anticipation. I couldn't get home fast enough. When I drove through Maine, I saw a Harley Davidson dealership. I knew Damon owned a 1981 Harley, and so I stopped and picked up a T-shirt for him. I drove straight to the garage to give him the shirt before I went home to unpack the van. He asked me, "You came straight here?" I replied, "Yes." In that moment he took my face in his hands and kissed me. Even with all the stories I had heard about fireworks going off the first time you kiss someone, that had never happened to me until this moment. I don't know how to explain it, but it felt even beyond the stories. Maybe I was super-charged from ceremonies, but when he kissed me, fireworks went off and I was completely shaken. I think the force and shock of it caught the two of us by surprise. I don't remember exactly what we said after that, but we made vague plans for him to come help me plant some trees the next day. I was so freaked out that I just went home without saying anything else about the kiss or our date.

Neither of us called each other for a couple of days. When I was over the shock and nervousness that came with the kiss, I finally picked up the phone and called him. When he answered, I asked him if he could still come over and help me plant the trees. I could hear relief in his voice over the phone. He had been waiting for me.

Damon came over and helped me in the garden the next day. We got everything planted and then he left. I thought I was home alone for the evening, but a little while later I got a phone call from Damon, asking if I wanted to go for ice cream. We went for sundaes and then watched a movie when we got back that night. We made plans to get together the next day to go for a ride on his Harley.

At this point I began to realize I was getting shy and nervous, and I wasn't sure what to do about the plans for the next day. We had never set a time or made any more solid plans than just going for the ride. He didn't call me, and I didn't call him, but then he just showed up on the bike at around two o'clock. He took me for a two-hour ride. When I got on the back of the bike behind him I had a sense of total trust and comfort. I felt deep joy and a complete sense of peace as we went riding through back roads. He dropped me off when we were done riding and he went home, but then called a little while later to ask if I enjoyed the ride. We went right out for another date the next night, for dinner. I kept telling myself "this can't be real" and "it feels too right," but after that night at dinner I saw him every day from then on.

Eventually I moved in with him, into his family's eighteenth-century homestead, complete with a cranberry bog, huge fields, and a beautiful old house. Through him and his past relationship, I was given an instant family with six grandchildren. Since then the number of grandchildren has grown to seven. I never had children in this life, but my seven grandchildren and my nieces and nephews fill that emptiness inside me. Because of Damon and his family, and the love that they surround me with, I have such a sense of fulfillment now in all areas of my life.

As I have grown through the years, I have finally achieved an understanding of a love so comfortable that it supports me in being who I am. It supports me in being my most creative self. I have a partner who is my grounding cord so that I can fly. This has been the greatest gift of love. There are no accidents. Your life is crafted by you and God before you are born, and God continues to walk with you through your life and through all the trials you have to face. Faith is learned through these trials, and also through all of our relationships; both relationships that are extremely hard and relationships that are loving and last through multiple lifetimes. This is how and why we're guided by love in life. Love transcends anything you have to fear, any obstacle you have to face, any trial you have to overcome. This final love that I have found is how my faith shows itself to me, and as I feel this love and faith support me, I feel Creator's love and support through every moment life offers, in all my relationships and in all the recesses of my soul. This journey from learning to use my gifts to finding Damon is where I have learned faith. This is where I have come to know God.

It's been more than 10 years that we've been together and it seems to have gone by so quick. It must be the life full of love that seems to accelerate time. Never in this lifetime have I known a time of such joy. Then I think, it has taken me lifetimes to find this place of peace. But did it really need to be this hard? Maybe I can see this peace as a sign that we really are to the point where we are changing our world. Maybe we are helping to create a world of compassion, tolerance, and love, in spite of all that has transpired in the past. Maybe the goodness of people and their love will win out over the way the world is portrayed by the media and politicians, focusing on the things that divide us. I pray that this is so.

Our family comes together daily in a unified effort; a combination of love and practicality, play and hard work, and each day this happens I see my dream realized. I watch my family gather together, young and old, to help mow the fields and bring in the bales of hay that will feed our horses. I watch my grandchildren work with their father in the garden for the food that will feed us this coming year. I think, "I could never have imagined such a paradise in my life." For this is paradise to me. I watch the girls in the garden picking strawberries, and know they are being raised to understand the earth, her natural laws and the bounty she provides, and how to live life in balance. Sometimes I will have a flashback to times before, and then I truly think this is right, like how I remember the old way to be, and I have hope. I have hope for my grandchildren and I have hope for all of us.

the vortex                                    2017

*I heard the voice of God this morning, telling me that I was one of the bright lights that he put on the planet in a very dark time, and that it was time for me to go out into the world to shine my light even brighter and teach all that I've learned. Teach and show the world so they can understand. I felt a great love and peace surround me.*

# we are still here

H unting in the woods of Maine with my dad is always a special time for me. I am away from computers and technology, and I can sit in prayer and meditation all day in the healing woods. Hunting is a spiritual experience for me. I first started hunting deer in my early thirties, and the first time I sat in the Maine woods I heard my Native grandfather say to me, *"Listen first to the silence. Then listen to what breaks the silence."*

Before every hunting trip I have a ceremony for the spirit of the deer that may offer itself to my family for our continued survival. I am in gratitude and deep thanks whenever I take a deer, and I cry every time. It is bittersweet knowing its spirit is being honored by me and it is not just another animal murdered and put on the shelf of a butcher shop or grocery store with no thought to the life it led. Each time I do these prayers to honor that particular animal's spirit, I feel a connection so deep that it seems to reach into my past and help me to remember.

We are still here. We, the red souls, have returned to heal our mother the earth and to heal what has been done to all indigenous people. We are still here. We have been reborn, and we are gathering. We want to put an end to the destruction of "Colonialism." We will put an end to the disappearing of Native peoples for the sake of money and greed, the same pattern that has been recurring for generations, from Wounded Knee to Standing Rock.

For many years, I have been involved in an organization that raises money for Indigenous communities all over the world. All the vendors have become close-knit friends and we can tell you many stories. At an event last summer, my dear friend came over to my booth to tell me that a customer of hers, not understanding Native culture or current events, had started a conversation with her, saying with conviction how he would have fought to help the Native people had he lived "back in the day!" She politely suggested he may want to "help" now with some of the current struggles we are facing. In that moment, he said in all seriousness, "No need. The Indians are all dead now!" She was shocked by his ignorance and reminded him that she was Native and standing right there, alive and in front of him. The message did not seem to sink in as he walked away from her.

Even in this time, we are not acknowledged. As we gather to have our voices heard, as we come together to pray, our prayers are still misunderstood. What happened at Standing Rock, ND[1] cannot be undone. It has set energy in motion. I had written most of this book before the events at Standing Rock occurred, and their message was just starting to surface. That event shook me to the core and awakened me further and more deeply. How can blatant, illegal actions still be perpetrated on our Mother Earth by corporations motivated by greed, which still control much of our natural resources? I am proud of the conviction and bravery shown to the world by our Water Protectors.

The channels I received for this book speak about healing what's been done to indigenous people all over this planet, and healing the destruction of our earth and our ways. Most don't even realize that in a country that boasts of religious freedom, our Native ceremonies were illegal until 1978![2]

As I watched what unfolded in the Dakotas through the eyes of my dear ones — my relatives that were there — and then witnessed the colonialist lies being blatantly told about the same events on news channels, I became very distraught. How could this still be happening? As I write the last chapter of this book, I realize that much of the country simply doesn't understand that indigenous people are still here.

While the Water Protectors at Standing Rock made their last stand, and I watched the dismantling of the camps at gunpoint through the live feeds broadcast by my dear friends who were there, I prayed harder than I have ever prayed before. Prayers from those that are already "awake" are what is needed to shift the consciousness of those that are asleep. The strong prayers of our indigenous ceremonies, or prayer with the strength of the rosary, or other ceremonies of prayer of other religions are what is needed to choose the side of right and goodness for all humanity.

When you live in service to others, from the heart, your work transcends the corrupt system that currently controls society, and which we have all witnessed. This system values the short-term gain of a few over the long-term gain for the collective.

It allows water to be taken over, bought and sold when we need it to survive. Jesus describes faith as 'the life-giving water' in the bible, and from my perspective there is no difference between that and the physical water that gives us life. Certain interests are buying up every fresh water source in this country because this is the next major commodity through which they will make money. This echoes the same story, and many similar stories, of the arrogant settler taking land and resources that did not belong to him. Taking sacred land and raping it for the pure profit of a few while risking the water and lives of thousands is no different than indiscriminately killing for one's personal gain. And whether or not people realize it, ignoring the Native and indigenous peoples' cry for help to protect water, earth, and this country means that we are complicit; we allow it to happen. So many have asked what can I do? I tell them to pray and they look at me confused. They don't realize it is that simple. Certainly another way to help is to raise your own voice with them, to listen, and to engage in activism to stop it. And you absolutely can do that, if you're able and willing. But if not, at the very least, pray. Heal yourselves. As we each heal one by one, we heal the collective and we heal our earth.

Your soul already knows that this current lifetime is your best opportunity to heal yourself, clear past karma, and create the life of which you've only dreamed, for you and those you love. The life you want is available to you in the time that we live in right now, in this moment. Life is bigger than you can see, bigger than what you believe to be your reality. Have the courage to go higher and see the life you are living from a different vantage point. Have the courage to face your past, have the courage to face your fears, and have the courage to face your future. Advance your own soul further than you thought possible and further than you've ever been. Doing this for yourself creates an opportunity for all of us to heal the karma of our past, and to heal the trauma of oppression and genocide that has been imposed on some for the profit and advancement of others. We need this healing and understanding so that our future is not a repetition of our past. We CAN break the cycle of generational trauma. As individuals and as a collective, humanity has the opportunity in this moment to leave a better world for our children and for the next seven generations. You must only have the courage to remember. This is why you're here, why you have reincarnated in this time to be here, why this book is in your hands! We are the ones our grandmothers and grandfathers prayed for, and we are the ones who have come to heal our world!

*We are still here.*

# RESOURCES

[1]*Standing Rock, ND 2016-2017, see for reference: http://standwithstandingrock.net/supporters/; http://standwithstandingrock.net/category/news/ or watch: Awake, a Dream from Standing Rock.*

[2]*"During the 1970s Congress investigated allegations that Indian religious practices were being severely disrupted, often unintentionally, by state and federal laws and by the actions of government officials. The House of Representatives issued a report that substantiated these claims. The report found that Indians were often prevented from visiting their sacred sites, denied the use of religious sacraments, and kept from performing services in their traditional manner. The report recommended that Congress take measures to protect Indian religious practices from unnecessary government interference. In 1978 Congress passed a joint resolution to this effect, the American Indian Religious Freedom Act (AIRFA). The act, as with all joint resolutions, contains no penalty provision that can be enforced against violators. However, AIRFA declares a policy that Congress has pledged to pursue... Sadly, AIRFA has not been very effective due to the absence of a penalty provision." —Stephen L. Pevar, The Rights of Indians and Tribes: The Basic ACLU Guide to Indian and Tribal Rights, 1992, see for reference: https://www.nlm.nih.gov/nativevoices/timeline/545.html*

# ACKNOWLEDGMENTS

There are always too many to thank when your entire life has been touched by so many. I have to start by thanking my ancestors and Spirit grandfather; in this process I have grown in all ways and with your continued guidance, I trust.

To my partner, my true love, and to my cousin, my true sister, thank you both for your unending patience and love on a day-to-day basis. No matter what I face in my life, I know you have my back and I have the courage to keep moving forward because your love surrounds me.

To my parents, and ALL my family, friends, Native sisters and brothers, I am grateful for the roles you each play in my life. I truly feel that *my tribe* has once again gathered together around me in various ways.

To Jayne, my dear friend, your unique gift helped me heal and I am forever grateful for you in my life.

To Joseph, my editor, you know this book would not have happened without you. Your patience, love and hard work is as much a part of this book as mine.

To Roberta, your support, wisdom, encouragement, and strength in my life have been there from the moment we met and through the many roles we have each played in the other's lives — this one and previous — and for this, my gratitude is endless.

Thank you Tina, your hand-holding and encouragement helped me throughout this process.

Thank you Michael G., for your initial and continued encouragement to listen to my ancestors and follow through on what was being asked of me even though I had no idea where to start.

To Charisse, my soul sister and saving grace, the spirits have truly brought us together, thank you!

*Oelalin* — *thank you* to everyone who has helped and supported me on my spiritual journey and has shared your wisdom through the years. I hold you all in my heart and in high regard.

*To my ancestors, angels, spirit guides, I ask that you please continue to guide my words, thoughts and deeds this day and every day for the good of all and harm to none. Emset Nogmag — We are all related.*

Printed in the United States
By Bookmasters